# A Ghost's Memoir

# A Ghost's Memoir

## The Making of Alfred P. Sloan's *My Years with General Motors*

John McDonald

The MIT Press
Cambridge, Massachusetts
London, England

This book was set in Sabon by Achorn Graphic Services, Inc., and was printed and bound in the United States of America.

Library of Congress Cataloging-in-Publication Data

McDonald, John.
  A ghost's memoir : the making of Alfred P. Sloan's "My years with General Motors" / John McDonald.
    p.  cm.
  Includes index.
  ISBN 0-262-13410-1 (hc. : alk. paper)
  1. Sloan, Alfred P. (Alfred Pritchard), 1875–1966. My years with General Motors. 2. General Motors Corporation—Management—History. 3. Automobile industry and trade—United States—Management—Case Studies. 4. Industrial management—United States—Case Studies. I. Title.

HD9710.U54 G47467   2002
338.7′6292′0973—dc21
                                        2001052195

# Contents

Acknowledgments   vii

Foreword: Who Was John McDonald? by Dan
Seligman   ix

I   The Making of *My Years with General Motors*   1

II  Suppression   73

III Publication   175

Epilogue   191

Index   193

# Acknowledgments

John McDonald finished this book five months before he died in December of 1998 at the age of 92. He had spent several years working on it, and it was an important project for him. Conversation about work and books and life was a way of being for John, and we his daughters often discussed this project with him. Many people helped him and us along the way. In the last year of work on the manuscript, when John could no longer see, several people served as his eyes for editorial revision: Diana Bush, Josh Schwartz, Pat and Ron Nicholson, Heather White, Daisy Walker, and Gina Fuentes Walker. Steven Brams, a friend admired for his work on game theory, took the manuscript to MIT Press and caught their interest. Lois Malone did additional editing of the manuscript based on the extensive annotations made by John in his final draft. Nancy Weschler provided judicious advice. Alfred Chandler gave generously of his knowledge of business in general and the history of negotiations about *My Years with General Motors* in particular. Ben Camardi, John's agent, was unflagging in his advocacy. To all of these people, we are very grateful.

We dedicate the publication of this book to our sons in the memory of their grandfather: Lucas Miller, Adam Vance, and Jacob Vance.

Joan McDonald Miller
Christie McDonald

# Foreword: Who Was John McDonald?

Dan Seligman

This is a book about a lawsuit—an unbelievable suit, brought by an amazing man (the book's author) against the world's then-largest corporation (General Motors). A bare-bones outline of the story would read something like this:

First, John McDonald works over a span of years (1954–1959) ghostwriting the memoirs of Alfred P. Sloan, Jr.—the man whose business strategies enabled General Motors to overtake seemingly invincible Ford and come to dominate the automobile industry in the 1920s and 1930s.

Second, General Motors tries to suppress this work. With publication by Doubleday only months away, GM tells Sloan that he dare not publish—that the manuscript he and McDonald have created could become evidence against the company in a possibly impending antitrust suit. Sloan unhappily complies with the company's demand. The book appears to be dead.

Third, McDonald sues GM for suppressing the book.

Fourth, GM caves in, agrees to publication, and the work is in the bookstores in the spring of 1964. Over the years, it has become a classic and is still required reading in business schools. Translated into many languages, it has apparently sold over a million copies. A few years ago, it was hailed by Bill

Gates as "probably the best book to read if you want to read only one book about business."

The bare bones, still not well known, seem fascinating in themselves. What makes this account irresistible are the details—the endless thrust and parry of the long war between John McDonald and GM—and the personalities implicated in the action. It is obviously no routine matter for a lone writer without major resources to take on the mightiest corporation in the world and make it back down. What is truly marvelous is the strategic thinking that made it possible for John to do this. In some ways, this "book about the book" is eerily parallel to the Sloan original. In both instances, we get a hard look at the strategic alternatives as they looked to the players at the time, and in this work, as in Sloan's *My Years with General Motors,* we see victory as emanating from deeply thought-out strategies. John beat down GM not by screaming or theatrics, but by out-thinking the company at every step of the way—as Sloan's GM had out-thought Ford decades earlier.

The story recounted in these pages has an extraordinary cast of characters. On center stage much of the time is Alfred Sloan himself: Sloan the business genius who basically created General Motors, long the world's largest and most successful corporation. Other major players are Henry R. Luce, founder of Time Inc.—the *Time-Life-Fortune-*etc. publishing empire—and his formidable brother-in-law, Maurice T. (Tex) Moore. Time Inc. nowadays is a relatively minor part of AOL Time Warner, but in the period described here, it was a uniquely dominant publishing colossus, and the men who ran it were national figures. Moore had been chairman of Time Inc., was still a director and corporate counsel, remained a senior partner of Cravath, Swaine, and Moore (the law firm retained by both GM and Time Inc.), and, on top of everything else, was now the personal lawyer of both Luce and Sloan. When GM demanded suppression, Moore became an implacable enemy of the book. Not surprisingly, given that a lawsuit is at the center of McDonald's story, other lawyers abounded. Among the heavyweights were Herbert Brownell, formerly Attorney General of the United States (in the Eisenhower administration); Daniel Boone, a GM lawyer who actually was a descendant of the famous pioneer, and who played a major role in ending the suppression effort; and Edward J. Ennis, then soon to become chairman of the American Civil Liberties Union, but shown here as McDonald's principal lawyer.

The portraits of these varied figures are neatly etched in this book. McDonald has an eye for the striking detail, and it is hard to think of anything more striking than the vignette of stiff-collar Alfred Sloan relaxing in a Palm Beach casino with high-rolling Walter Chrysler.

One figure who is not adequately captured is John McDonald himself. McDonald, who died in December 1998 at 92, was an utter original. Alas, he was also utterly modest. It takes a lot of nerve and audacity to sue General Motors—and at one point John was close to suing his bosses at Time Inc., as well. Yet he seemed wary of writing about himself. It just didn't come naturally. Readers following his narrative will rapidly sense that this was a man of high seriousness and deep intelligence. But they might get more out of the story if they had a more rounded view of its protagonist. At his memorial service I said that he had made life more interesting for just about everybody who crossed his path, and I wasn't exaggerating. In any case, I hope to flesh out some details about the author here.

I first met him one night in April 1950, at approximately 3 A.M., on the fiftieth floor of the Empire State Building. We were both there for the same reason: We were both writers on the

*Fortune* staff, were both creating articles that had slipped their deadlines, and were both working around the clock in an effort to catch up. When we made contact in the dark, and each of us had reassured himself that the other guy wasn't a prowler, we began to chat. A half-century later, I remember vividly the instant awareness that I was dealing with someone out of the ordinary.

John had this effect on quite a few people, as evidenced by the range and catholicity of his acquaintances. At one time or another, he was close not only to the business titan who had put together General Motors but also to Leon Trotsky, with whom he had spent time in Mexico three years before Trotsky's assassination there. Sloan and Trotsky—a more antipodal pair is hard to imagine. Our author's other good friends included poet/novelist Robert Penn Warren, mathematician and game-theorist John von Neumann, real-estate impresario William Zeckendorf, photographer Walker Evans, theatrical producer Roger Stevens, and numerous icons from the world of horse-racing. In our years together on *Fortune,* I observed that most of the staff writers, including me, would go off and write about some large corporation, then typically lose touch with its senior people. When John went off on an assignment, it recurrently resulted in chief executive officers wishing to stay in touch with him. His friendships with race-horse owners led to his becoming, I believe, the only *Fortune* writer to hold a press pass at New York's Aqueduct and Belmont racetracks.

McDonald was a gambler. Before meeting him, it had never occurred to me that a truly serious person could also be a gambler, but John plainly was both. His gambling had been manifested at numerous racetracks since the 1930s, and when the thoroughbreds were not running, he was willing to take on the trotters and, if necessary, the greyhounds or even (if in Florida) jai alai. I was with him on a certain number of these occasions, and also hosted a high-stakes poker game in which he was a star participant for years. John being John, a fair number of the people he dealt with as a journalist ended up in the game, my own favorite being a hard-drinking, merciless opponent named Chester Davis, who had the arguably good fortune to be Howard Hughes's chief lawyer.

In John's early years, the major intellectual themes in his life revolved around far-left politics. Not long after he arrived in New York during the threadbare 1930s (he was living on $5 a week at one point), he was deeply involved in radical causes, always with an anti-Stalinist component. He was one of the featured players in Alan M. Wald's 1987 book, *New York Intellectuals: The Rise and Decline of the Anti-Stalinist Left from the 1930s to the 1980s.*

Later in life, his intellect ranged far more widely. Influenced by his wife Dorothy and daughter Joan McDonald Miller, he became a strenuous advocate of abstract expressionist painting. Influenced by his other daughter, Christie, who is a professor of romance languages and literature at Harvard, he was endlessly poking around in French literary and philosophical issues. He wrote scholarly works about the origins of fly-fishing. Having talked *Fortune*'s editors into assigning him an article on poker, he began with the heavily mathematical *Theory of Games and Economic Behavior,* by von Neumann and Oskar Morgenstern. This led to a decades-long fascination with game theory, about which John became enormously knowledgeable. He produced one major work, *The Game of Business,* which applied game-theoretic principles to the strategic problems of J. Paul Getty, Walt Disney, Howard Hughes, and others. A cherished favorite of my own is a slender volume he was producing just about the time I first met him. Its title: *Strategy in Poker, Business, and*

*War.* As evidenced in his moves during the suit against General Motors, game theory came to permeate his thinking.

I claim to have had something to do with the origins of the present book. Not a lot, but something. While the war with GM was on—this would be 1959 to 1963—I had an overpowering sense, every time I was updated by John, that the story of the suppression effort was just too good to keep secret. Over something like a quarter-century, long after the Sloan book had been published, I continued nagging at him to sit down and write an account of what had happened. John certainly did not dispute that he had been at the center of a fascinating episode in American corporate history, but he resisted undertaking any serious effort to tell the tale.

At least he did until April 1990. When the April 23 issue of *Fortune* appeared, everything changed.

This issue contained a long article by Peter Drucker that, it emerged, would form the introduction to a new edition of Sloan's *My Years with General Motors,* to be published by Doubleday/Currency. The publication was remarkable on several counts. Although John had written the book, and retained a 50 percent royalty interest in its sales, the publisher had never apprised him that a new edition was coming along. A far more serious matter: It had not bothered to check Peter Drucker's account of the book's history.

Drucker is a serious, wide-ranging, highly original thinker who commands enormous respect—and, for the most part, deserves it. Having occasionally edited his articles for Fortune, I had become one of his many fans. But I found his ruminations on the Sloan book ludicrous, at several levels.

He writes in his introduction: "*My Years with General Motors* was written primarily to rebut—or at least to counterbalance—a book that Sloan thought to be pernicious: my book on General Motors, *Concept of the Corporation.*" Readers of McDonald's early chapters will see that this is simply not true. The book that John ghostwrote grew out of a much smaller project, originally intended to state some basic management principles in an article for *Fortune.* The project kept growing, even as it was endlessly redefined by both John and Sloan, and finally became a book. The main purpose of the book was not to talk back to Drucker or anybody else, but to set down, in detail, the strategies that had enabled GM to prevail.

Drucker's introduction features some ghastly factual mistakes. One passage tells us that Sloan, who was childless, had been crushed by the death of his younger brother Raymond— a substitute child, in Drucker's affecting rendition of the tale. (He quotes Sloan as saying that Raymond's death while in his fifties was "the greatest personal tragedy in my life.") Here a serious difficulty is the fact that Raymond died in 1983, seventeen years after Alfred, and in the book itself Alfred refers to him as still living.

But Drucker's major problems were in another area. He had evidently heard that there had been long delays in getting the book published, but he (a) had the dates mixed up and (b) was wildly wrong about the reasons for the delay. The book, he said, "was substantially finished in 1954, yet not published until ten years later." In fact, only three chapters were written as late as 1956—the year when Sloan and McDonald took this material to Doubleday, looking (successfully, as it turned out) to make a sale. The book was not close to being finished until 1959, the year in which General Motors launched the suppression effort.

And why was the book delayed? It appears that neither Drucker nor his editors at Doubleday knew anything about the suppression effort, or about McDonald's suit to end it. According to Drucker's introduction in the 1990 edition, the ten-year delay was triggered by Sloan himself, who "refused to publish as long as any of the GM people mentioned in the book was still alive." Why would he do this? Apparently because he was enormously kind-hearted, felt that some of the executives who were still living might be offended by certain passages in the book, and, accordingly, held up publication until the last of them died. Says Drucker: "On the day of the death of the last living person mentioned in the book, Sloan released it for publication."

This was absurd. For openers, it is inconceivable that a man in his eighties would refuse to publish a book until he had outlived all his colleagues. Nor would it make sense to let the book be published posthumously on any such grounds, because there was next to nothing in it that could be construed as denigrating any GM managers. And on the evidence of the book as published, Sloan was engaging in no such fantasies. In his preface to the original edition, and every subsequent edition, including the one being introduced by Drucker, Sloan gives credit to fourteen colleagues who had helped on the book and were still alive when it first came out; in virtually every case, they were not only "mentioned" in *My Years with General Motors,* but played prominent roles in Sloan's account. It boggles the mind that Drucker, not to mention Doubleday's editors, failed to notice this huge discrepancy between Drucker's introduction and—only a few pages away—Sloan's preface.

In April 1991, when he had read through the new edition, John McDonald sent a letter to Doubleday/Currency editor Harriet Rubin, pointing up these anomalies and absurdities, and expressing surprise that at no point in the creation of this edition had the publisher thought to contact the author about it. The letter was never answered.

But by this time, John had decided that the story of *My Years with General Motors* really did need to be told. We are all the richer for this decision.

# I

## The Making of *My Years with General Motors*

On March 4, 1959, Mr. Sloan called me into his office. I sat down beside him at the corner of his desk, as I had done a great many times in the past several years. He then made an announcement which, if effective, would wipe out the record of his genius as the longtime head and developer of General Motors. With it would also go the core of the internal history of that corporation.

He said: "John, we are not publishing."

In the courtesies of address across our generations, he— Alfred P. Sloan Jr., a very formal man out of the nineteenth century whose graven face was surrounded by the collar which had once seemed to hold up his chin, but had come down over time—he was Mr. Sloan and I was John; few and only those from far back called him Alfred. We observed this decorum faithfully, and I maintain it here.

A distractedness in his voice, then rare for him, conveyed a sense that he was as shocked as I at what he was saying. For after four and a half years of work together with Catharine Stevens, the project's manager, and her substantial staff, we were thirty days from the delivery of a manuscript of the memoir of Mr. Sloan's life at General Motors—the book's working title was then *The General Motors Story*, later changed to *My Years with General Motors*—to Doubleday for fall publication.

Not publishing? That was hard to believe.

Mr. Sloan said: "They say it will destroy General Motors." "They" were the lawyers for General Motors.

"How?" I asked.

His composure giving way further, he answered: "I don't know. You talk to them."

I didn't think that at arm's length, a distance I would have to keep, they would tell me what they had not told him.

He said resignedly: "What can you do when they say you've got cancer?"

I protested his part in stopping publication.

He said dryly, his composure restored: "Complain to the right parties."

I understood his drift: The book would "destroy" General Motors by disclosing violation of antitrust law, the remedy for which would be the forced breakup of the corporation into two or more parts. The violation: excessive growth in market share, which metaphorically suggested "cancer" to the man who with Charles Kettering was a major backer of the American cancer research taking place at the Sloan-Kettering Cancer Center in New York. He took no blame for canceling the book and directed me to "the right parties." Unknowingly he had sketched the future of the book.

The continued existence of General Motors as an entity producing more than half of the automobiles in North America was in fact in jeopardy at this time. Prosecutors from the antitrust division of the Justice Department had recently called a grand jury to consider indicting the corporation for violation of laws against monopoly. They had been investigating General Motors for several years, and had recently requested documents going back to 1929 from the corporation's files. General Motors' defense was in the hands of a team headed by Bruce ("Judge") Bromley from the distinguished New York law firm Cravath, Swaine, and Moore. Another senior member and future presiding partner of that firm, Maurice T. ("Tex") Moore, was chairman and chief counsel of Time Inc. (now AOL Time Warner) and Mr. Sloan's personal lawyer. He had brought Mr. Sloan the message that instigated this cancellation of the publication of the book. These individuals and their institutions would play major parts in the fight that would take place over the unpublished book.

Mr. Sloan was a legend in the automobile industry, one of its original participants in the United States from around the turn of the century. He had worked with as well as socialized with Walter Chrysler, and had passed evenings with Henry Ford in the club car of the New York–Detroit Wolverine during the teens of the century. Ford was then an outstanding businessman and Mr. Sloan's largest customer for his Hyatt Roller Bearings. Without overweening personal ambition, Mr. Sloan came out on top of General Motors and superseded Ford to take the company to the top of the industry; he is remembered as a managerial genius. Mr. Sloan looked back on all this while working on his memoir, believing he had done the right thing—and now that it was done he found himself told he was in the wrong.

What was at stake in the book as the alleged destroyer of General Motors was not the jobs of 600,000 employees nor necessarily the values of the stockholders, which "corporate raiders" would say could be improved by the breakup of General Motors. For this was before the takeover era, in the time of corporate loyalties in the United States. From the 1920s through the 1960s, such loyalty was a jealously held value and a factor in business strategies, creating resistance to the mergers and takeovers that have become common today. Mr. Sloan's predicament was his being caught between the values represented in the book—personal values and the values of General Motors—on the one hand, and the perception of these values on the part of his own and General Motors' lawyers on the other. They wanted to destroy his book to save General Motors from the burning issues of the time: big business and monopoly. And they had the power to attempt to do so.

## 1948–1954

The book that the lawyers thought so threatened General Motors dealt with Mr. Sloan's business life, beginning with his graduating from MIT in the Class of 1895 as an engineer. The book described Mr. Sloan's entry into the automobile business through the manufacture of roller bearings, and covered his career at General Motors from 1918. It had its origins in conversations I had had with him in the late 1940s and early 1950s, when he was already thinking about how to resolve the potential conflict between the great growth of General Motors and the antitrust laws then presumed able to restrain that growth beyond some percentage share of the automobile market. Political opposition to the phenomenon of large corporations and their influence on public affairs was of course also on his mind. Hearings were then being held in Washington by a "Senate Subcommittee on the Concentration of Economic Power." As the largest industrial corporation in the United States and first on the Fortune 500 since that ranking had begun, General Motors was a target on both counts. The book had been my idea, but Mr. Sloan had had a lot of nerve to undertake such a disclosure of corporate information in the first place.

I had been a writer at *Fortune* for three years when, one day in 1948, I called Mr. Sloan's office to request an interview for an article I was writing on General Motors' diesel engines. He agreed to see me, on his own as it turned out. I had only to walk across the street from my office in the old Time and Life Building to his private suite at 30 Rockefeller Plaza. I found him sitting in modest grandeur behind his desk. His austere visage was lined and ruddy with aging life, and quite familiar from photographs. A vase of fresh mixed flowers stood off to the side. He rose to greet me in a courtly manner and with a Brooklyn accent that was uniquely New York.

"You want to talk about diesel engines?" he asked. Mr. Sloan was happy to talk about diesel engines, and unworried at having won a nearly absolute monopoly in diesel locomotives with an engine that had been developed by Charles Kettering, General Motors' chief of research. After having bought two small locomotive companies, General Motors had developed diesel-powered locomotives with such success that they knocked the big duopoly of steam locomotives—Baldwin and American—out of the market. As diesel locomotives represented economic (though not in everyone's mind aesthetic) progress, General Motors appeared to be relatively safe for a while as sole possessor of that market.

Mr. Sloan liked the emphasis his locomotive story gave to performance—that is, in economists' terms, expanded products, lower costs and prices, and steady output across time—over market share, or what is often called the "structure" of markets. But Mr. Sloan was a realist and the next time we met, in 1949, to discuss the Sherman Antitrust Act banning agreements and monopoly, about which I was then writing a piece, he talked about accepting a ceiling on General Motors' share of the postwar automobile market, which was being strongly revived at the time.

"General Motors," he said, according to my notes, "would like to get back the percentage of the automobile business it had before the war." He said that General Motors would take a ceiling of 40–45 percent and grow relative to the total growth of the economy. If the economy grew as he expected—and he was quite prescient about the potential for economic growth—the ceiling on the General Motors share of the market would not interfere, he thought, with the dynamics of efficiency and growth in the operation of the business. He was more concerned with the populist politics against big business than with the antitrust issue of market share. "Bigness," he observed, "is unrelated to the Sherman Act." And he said, "I don't believe business [generally] will get any bigger in relation to the size of the country. The limiting factor here is government policy, which may slow up the rate of progress."

Mr. Sloan's willingness in 1949 to put a ceiling on General Motors' share of the automobile market in spite of his preference for performance as the test of a competitive market was the result, presumably, of his realization that it was possible that an antitrust suit would be brought by the Justice Department—likely, if General Motors gained close to or more than half the American car market. Later General Motors did in fact gain more than half the market, and as noted, in 1954 the Justice Department started an antitrust investigation of the corporation.

As Mr. Sloan had a lot to say out of experience and was facing the issue of monopoly in practice, I urged him in 1949 and thereafter to write about it from the perspective of a businessman. He said he would like to try, and he had the time. He had chosen to resign as chief executive of General Motors in 1946, and though still Chairman of the Board and of the Finance Committee and a power in the corporation, his responsibilities there were limited to participating in policy-making decisions and top executive appointments. His attentions to the Sloan Foundation, the Sloan-Kettering Medical Center, and the MIT School of Industrial Management (later to be renamed the Sloan School of Management) had not filled the gap. Mr. Sloan had moved his office from the old General Motors building in New York to a suite in Rockefeller Center, and he came to this office from his nearby Fifth Avenue apartment every day. He sat behind his desk and read the current data on automobile production and sales that filled its top right drawer much as an orchestra director would pore over a musical score. He was always available for a conversation, and we had a good many. I convinced the managing editor of *Fortune* to publish an article he had written on "big business." I was to assist him with the article editorially.

On May 26, after several discussions in early 1950, Mr. Sloan wrote me a rather formal letter confirming his resolve to write, with my assistance, an article for *Fortune*. The article would be on, as he put it, "the effectiveness of large-scale enterprise using the performance of General Motors as an example. ..." He added that pending litigation involving General Motors meant that his article would need the approval of the legal department. The litigation was the government's antitrust suit against the Du Pont company alleging that, as a supplier, Du Pont got too much of the paint business from General Motors while also owning a controlling interest in the company and being represented on its Board of Directors. Despite the hazard, he agreed to proceed.

In July of 1950, Mr. Sloan wrote me asking for a delay. He thought that people would not be interested in his article, given the outbreak of the Korean war. The next deadline was to have been July 1, 1951, but on May 15 he wrote: "I have been so tied up with all kinds of things that I think I must ask you for another month on that article. And this is the last time that I will ask you for the same."

By now he was into his version of writer's block, and we were into an editorial relationship. On June 29, 1951, he wrote:

I received your message about the article we have discussed for so long.

I just can't take the responsibility of a September issue because it is too important for me to do so. I have been constantly interrupted in my work on the article and have been delayed in getting some pertinent data that I felt belonged to the same. I plan to go down to Hot Springs the latter part of July to spend a month and while there devote my time exclusively to the article.

I hate to keep procrastinating because I am just as much interested in it as ever, but I think we will agree that it is not significant that it will be done one month as against another, and in Hot Springs where I will not be interrupted and can do the job I want to do and you want to have me do.

I replied on July 7, 1951 that I would find a place for his article in a later issue, and gave him a new manuscript date of September 1. He wrote back immediately: "I highly appreciate the consideration you are extending me in this job of mine which I admit I have not done very well. I hope to do better in the immediate future." But on September 26, at the end of a letter thanking him for his comments on a piece of mine on another subject, I could only comment: "When am I going to be your editor?" Indeed, in response to a standing invitation, I often gave him a call and dropped in. He was of course an excellent source for a journalist on business subjects, and so willing that for a couple of years he gave me more time contributing his knowledge to the needs of my work than I gave him on the writing end of his.

On January 22, 1952 I wrote to him: "Are you not still considering your own piece on big business?"

He was, and finally one day in the spring of 1953, he called me over and handed me a manuscript carrying the title: "Business Bigness and Bigness Efficiency," by Alfred P. Sloan, Jr. It was quite unsatisfactory as an article for *Fortune*, but in the rejection letter of June 29 I wrote him several thousand words of commentary. In summary: "It is too abstract and cold. It lacks concreteness, color, warmth of personality and the actual-

ity of your participation in the development of General Motors.
. . . It should be a great story. It should contain the genesis of
the ideas out of which General Motors was built. The main tests
that were met. . . ." And, I said, it should contain an account of
his own life in General Motors.

This was a pretty heavy load of editorial comment, and so
it was not surprising that my author came up with another
hitch. On September 1, 1953, he wrote:

I hate to write you along the following lines because I have disappointed you so often and have made so many comments about what
I might do and then have not done it. However, circumstances compel
me to say that it is just impossible for me to finish the article in time
for the issue that you mentioned when you were last here in my office.

I told you I was limited in the time I would put on it, by family
problems. Since you left on vacation I have had to face the loss of a
very close relative which has put me in a position, psychologically and
time-wise, where it is hard for me to concentrate on an abstract problem of this kind. However, I am working on it as best I can. I will be
able to send you two more chapters for criticism, within a few days,
so far as I can now foresee.

In addition to my own time factor, the story has got to go before
General Motors and I do not think that will present any difficulty, but
it will require a certain amount of time because all the people there
have so much to do. Therefore, let me say I will hammer away on it
because I am just as anxious to do the job as I can possibly be. I am
taking real pride in doing it and now that I have finally got started the
limitations mentioned above, cause me to write as I have.

I hope you are enjoying a fine vacation in Montana. You certainly
escaped a week or ten days of terrific heat—at least I suppose you
have—because I can't imagine it getting as hot in Montana as it is
here.

I replied from Montana on September 9 that we could set
another date—his article was subsequently taken off *Fortune*'s
tentative schedule for November or December of that year—
"when you have got far enough along to see your way." His
only policy problem that I knew about was the Du Pont case,

which was still in court and would be for years. It did not seem to me to be an obstacle, as Mr. Sloan had testified, and the whole trial record would be available. I urged him to proceed and in addition to the substantial comments I had written for him, I offered further editorial help. On November 2, I queried him: "How's your story coming?" But somewhere along the way the manuscript of his "Bigness" story acquired a subtitle— "A Proposed Message to the Stockholders of General Motors Corporation," by Alfred P. Sloan, Jr., Chairman. The article had turned into a corporate position paper, something in which I had no interest. As such, it disappeared from my view.

Mr. Sloan then changed the subject of discussion to the general question of what makes a good business executive, and he suggested the possibility of our undertaking "a comprehensive survey of what I am talking about." But despite his qualifications to lead such a study, I did not follow up on it. Theorizing was not Mr. Sloan's cup of tea, I reasoned, and his thoughts would be more interesting if tied to the real events of his business life.

In the early months of the new year, talks along this line, together with the negative comments I had made on his "Bigness" piece back in June of 1953, led to a new project that was quite different in conception from the failed article. This was the notion of a memoir by Mr. Sloan of his own experience in the automobile industry from its beginnings in the 1890s through his life in General Motors from 1918. It was of course a more ambitious project, and a larger one: The idea was to produce a book that could also spin off a series of pieces for *Fortune*. Ambitious as it was, Mr. Sloan wanted to do it, and for a while he made some tries, mainly thought-tries, that discouraged him. One day in the spring of 1954 he called me over and said that he could not complete the project without sub-

stantial professional help. He asked if I could recommend someone. I said I would look around.

I thought of the MIT economist M. A. Adelman, whose work
on large-scale business I had read and written about and whom
I had met at a seminar on antitrust policy in Cambridge in
1949.[1] His views of monopoly stressed performance over
"structure" and therefore paralleled Mr. Sloan's views, if origi-
nating in a somewhat different sort of mind. I thought they
could contribute something to each other. Mr. Sloan was willing, but Professor Adelman was occupied and declined, although he would later make an important contribution to the
project. Not getting anywhere with the search, I realized there
was a possibility of assisting Mr. Sloan myself.

My relations with Mr. Sloan up to this time, while on my
initiative, had been in the context of my capacity as a *Fortune*
writer and editor. At this point we had in common a desire to
get down on paper, to justify and to defend, the industrial history he and his company had made. I was interested in the record, the history, and the story of the automobile, so while our
interests may not have been identical, they certainly overlapped.
From my perspective, an accord was possible if he would abide
by accepted standards of writing history; in any case my liberal
views were entertaining to a large corporation conditioned by
antitrust law. As Carl Kaysen once observed, "the liberal creed
at that time put big business in a central place in its demonol-
ogy." And after years of conversations regarding the less ambitious article that had failed, we would be favored by a certain

---

1. This remarkable seminar included Lowell B. Mason, then an
astounding theorist of monopoly, Carl Kaysen, a then unknown Harvard fellow who would eventually become Oppenheimer's successor
as the head of the Institute for Advanced Studies, and M. A. Adelman
of MIT.

familiarity—important if I were to work with him on the book.

The idea of looking at the auto industry from the inside with Mr. Sloan was interesting to me personally. I was born in Detroit in 1906, soon after the automobile itself. The neighborhood, called Indian Village and West Village by its developers, was hardly settled then. The migration farther east to Grosse Pointe awaited the development of the automobile for transportation. I remember that at the age of three or so I saw the first Model T, parked across Champlain (now Lafayette) Street and down a way, which bore investigation. At that time, fire engines were still driven by wild-looking horses, and in the winter groceries were delivered across the snow by horse-drawn sleigh; but these horse-drawn vehicles were no older in my new eyes than the Model T. To grownups the automobile was a novelty; to me both automobile and horse-drawn wagon were part of the same variety show. As I grew up, automobile families—the Fords, the Dodges, the Fishers of Fisher Body, and many others—were everywhere around town and in the neighborhood. The Edsel Fords came to live two blocks away on East Jefferson Avenue, in a mansion with grounds that extended down to the Detroit River. Two little boys peered, invariably, through the grating. The mansion was later taken over by the United Automobile Workers for its Health Department, and the Edsel Fords moved to Grosse Point. Nearby, on Jefferson Avenue, lived the lawyer who drew up Henry Ford's first incorporation papers and in payment took, according to legend, the few shares of stock which eventually made him one of the many new automobile millionaires. Also across the avenue from the Edsel Fords were the Mendelsohns, who were the financial backers of the seven Fisher brothers of Fisher Body—which merged, in the 1920s, into General Motors. I knew a girl named

Graham whose father was Graham of the firm Graham-Paige. While running errands for my father's neighborhood drugstore I made deliveries of special interest to me—to the house on the river owned by C. Harold Wills, who was chief engineer at Ford when they designed the Model T. In 1920 Wills would design and build the Wills Saint Claire, always one of my favorite cars to look at. A sporty Wills roadster with disk wheels and a rumble seat for two usually sat in his driveway, and on my way to the house I would inspect it. I also remember years of cars, sometimes only their names, many of them made in Detroit, some—Hudson, Chalmers, Chrysler—made within a mile or so of my house, and others made not far away in Michigan and the Midwest. Most have since been lost to the vagaries of the economy and the strategies of the marketplace. The names sound the music of car-time: Dort, Maxwell, Saxon, Haynes, Stutz Bearcat, REO, and Olds—the later Oldsmobile, which was originally named for Mr. R. E. Olds—Hupmobile, Auburn, Briscoe, Overland (we had one), Studebaker (one of them, too, later), Scripps-Booth, Marmon, Chalmers, Paige, Sheridan, Nash, Essex, Hudson, Oakland, the weirdly named and expensive Locomobile, the enormous Packard-Twin Six, and the Pierce Arrow. And of course there were Fords, Chevrolets, Dodges (later Chrysler), Buicks, Lincolns, Cadillacs, and others. Where I grew up, royalty was a family whose name was also the name of a motorcar.

But it was not just nostalgic curiosity about the automobile that made the project intriguing. During the past nine years at *Fortune* I had done a good many long pieces on varied subjects mostly of my choosing—trout and salmon fishing, game theory, economic theory, the RAND Corporation (a progenitor of think tanks). I had written on a great number of industries and corporations—and *Fortune* had published what I had written for them. These articles took time and only the old monthly *Fortune* would have backed such costly work. It was a strain for a commercial magazine. *Fortune* had long featured "the corporation story," much as the *New Yorker* had the profile and the *Paris Review* "Writers at Work." My take on the corporation story was to give particular attention to strategic situations where individuals, institutions, and groups of various kinds interacted interdependently and thought in ways—both cooperatively and noncooperatively—that escaped common classical economic and decision theory. This concept of strategy came from game theory, which has become more widely known since 1994, when three game theorists received the Nobel prize in economics. With the help of its original developers, John von Neumann and Oskar Morgenstern, I had done studies in game theory and had written on the subject, for *Fortune* in 1949 and in the book *Strategy in Poker, Business, and War,* which was published by Norton in 1950. I thought I could do a good job on Sloan and General Motors somewhat along these lines if I had the materials. General Motors, although located at the center of American industrial power and prosperity, was secretive; Mr. Sloan, in our conversations, was not. So there would be discoveries. The book would contain something new. As for Mr. Sloan, he was an icon, not only of General Motors but of corporate America itself. I thought I could knock it off in a year.

## 1954–1956

I walked across the street to Mr. Sloan's office to ask him what he would think of my doing the book with him. He responded that he had been hoping that I would. We talked about arrangements, beginning with who would pay for it.

Mr. Sloan asked, "General Motors?"

"No."

"The Foundation?"

"No."

"Me?"

"Yes."

He smiled the smile of satisfaction which indicated that something in particular had pleased him. The book would be independent. We settled on a fee, and he proposed that I should take all the royalties: book, subsequent magazine serials, et cetera. I thought it better that he have an economic stake in the outcome, as a matter of discipline—he obviously didn't need the money—and so I proposed that we share all royalties fifty-fifty. He agreed. On the subject of credits, Mr. Sloan proposed that we should share them as coauthors. But I thought that while we expected to agree on the elements of a sound memoir, we could not expect to be of one mind about some other things—given particular attitudes, opinions, and such. In any case the subject of the book was his life, not mine, and therefore he alone should sign the book, take full responsibility, and leave no room for buck-passing. My responsibility would be for good history and for getting it down on paper; we could decide on my credit later and write into the book how it was done. We agreed on all that, and further that he had the right to cancel publication if he chose. It seemed to be a good, cooperative negotiation of interests. Mr. Sloan's lawyer would draft a letter of agreement for my lawyer to review.

The next time I heard from him was July 9, 1954. He wrote that his lawyer had found the matter "quite complicated," and added: "I am sure it is all right." Reading the American idiom "sure" as meaning not quite all right, I wrote him a query to which he replied on July 22: "I have your note of July 21st.

There is no complication around my decision as I have already made it, as outlined to you." The delay, he said, was due to the concerns of his "counsel" regarding taxes, but whatever came of that would make no difference to him: "I want to go on just the same."

The paragraph that followed contained an unexpected deviation from our oral agreement. Had I been able to "read" what it was telling me about the future, I would have recognized it as the ill omen that it was:

I am submitting to my counsel today, a copy of a proposed letter to you, largely on the lines of a memorandum handed to me by you. I shall undoubtedly have a favorable reply within a day or so, after which I will send the agreement to you for your criticism and acceptance, if satisfactory. The only change that I have made in the financial set up is in the 50% division on certain rights outlined in your memorandum. I have eliminated those relating to magazine publication. This, of course, eliminates *Fortune* and such other magazines as might use the manuscript, in whole or in part. This, I am sure, will not make much difference to you and I think it will be better although I am not insisting upon it if you feel very strongly about it.

Far from being the legendary crisp man of decision, Mr. Sloan was, when he chose to be, a master of ambivalence. He had described himself remarkably well in his testimony in the Du Pont suit: "It is generally my custom, when I get some resistance, to back out of it and try to do a selling job rather than to force the issue." And he said: "I have never had much respect for my own ability as a negotiator. I am too apt to look at two sides of the question." These observations would explain some critical events in the history of General Motors and should have alerted me—and him, too, in this instance—before we started.

The hard fact in his letter about the magazine rights, I soon learned, was that it was only I and not *Fortune* who was eliminated from the magazine rights. In his capacity as chairman of

Time Inc., Maurice T. Moore, who was also Mr. Sloan's lawyer, had negotiated an option on the magazine rights for Time
Inc. Thus, in deference to Moore, Mr. Sloan had eliminated me,
and while allowing me to insist on our agreement in this matter,
nevertheless stated his judgment in support of the change: "It
will not make much difference to you," he stated, "and I think
it will be better. . . ." It did make a difference to me, and it was
not clear why it was better for him or me: for him perhaps
taxwise; and he had been persuaded to deal directly with the
chairman of Time Inc. Mr. Sloan's soft words left it to me, if
I wished, to oppose his judgment and to confront my employer,
Time Inc. I was a free agent on leave from *Fortune* without pay,
and there never was any question but that *Fortune* (and Time
Inc. and *Life*) would get a magazine series from the Sloan book.
The issue was the royalties, in which I had a half-interest. I
could insist on the magazine royalty rights as agreed, or let them
go and hope that their value would come back to me by some
other route when I brought the serial out of the book to *Fortune*. Perhaps they would compensate me with a raise in salary.
I had a moment of misgiving about the whole project, with still
time to back out.

It is with the benefit of hindsight that I realize I should have
slugged it out, not only for the material value of the rights but
also to bring the relationships in and around the project—here,
Moore with his interests—out into the open. I can't remember
altogether why—whether it was weakness, prudence, or illu-
sion—but reluctantly I relinquished my share of the magazine
rights. After a couple of additional letters from Mr. Sloan regarding details, we signed an agreement on August 9, 1954,
and on October 1, after six years of acquaintance, we started
to work on the book from scratch. Catharine Stevens, whom
I found through the employment office of the Columbia

Graduate School, came to work with us and remained a major participant throughout the project. She took an office in Mr. Sloan's suite; I gave up my *Fortune* office and rented workshop space in a brownstone ten minutes or so away.

Catharine Stevens was a lucky find for Mr. Sloan and me. Forty years later, in March 1995, she sent me this recollection of how she came into it:

Some time in the fall of 1954 I was studying on the GI bill [she had been a WAVE in the war] and had registered at the employment office there to find part-time work, secretarial or other. Shortly after registering, I was called to work for one or two professors, taking dictation and transcribing the copy. I had a feeling that many applicants were available for typing, but not many knew shorthand nor editing when necessary. My next interview was with John McDonald, an editor and writer with *Fortune*. He was working with a business executive and wanted someone to transcribe the executive's talk from a tape recorder. Mr. McDonald explained that he and the executive would meet each day and give me the results of their work on the tape recorder. Mr. McDonald encouraged me to ask questions; the job sounded interesting and we came to terms. But after a while, I had a feeling that something was missing. I couldn't put my finger on it; but I felt I was too far apart from the two men and I was missing something I couldn't identify. So, I asked John McDonald if I could be in the room when they were working together. I thought I could do much better that way. I learned that their procedure was for Mr. Sloan to talk into the tape recorder, then occasionally stop and talk with John. The tape recorder was stopped when they were talking together. After their discussion, it would be turned on. It was those stops, which I must have felt unconsciously, that made me feel I was too far away. Mr. Sloan was very gracious in greeting me when I came into the room. That was an encouragement. Right from the beginning I felt comfortable with Mr. Sloan, as I had with John.

In December of 1954, I gave Mr. Sloan my first progress report, with a copy to the editors of *Fortune:* "In the first two months you produced an extensive text." That was raw text from dictation, about which I said, "This is a real accomplishment as to quantity and in good part as to quality; the sections relating to engineering and distribution, for example, are excellent, and the sections on organization, I think, are unique and brilliant." But we had a problem and it was teaching us about memory. Mr. Sloan drew on memories of his early years at General Motors, from 1918 into 1920, to criticize the founder and then head of General Motors, William C. Durant, in a way that denigrated him as a mere speculator; Mr. Sloan had a strong preference for producers of real goods over speculators. Eventually, when I showed him more information about Durant, he would considerably modify the bias in his memory. In the progress report this led on to other matters of importance for the whole book:

One thing in particular that I should like to mention for your consideration relates to you and Durant. Promoter that he was, he nevertheless brought General Motors into existence on a pattern of integration. This early integration was crude, motivated by financial speculation, full of dead branches, and in the end, so far as Durant was concerned, it didn't work. But there it was, a thing with shape for you to start with in 1921 (along with Du Pont capital). It seems possible then that your own unique contribution was [in] organization and growth. These are in fact, the two main themes of the American corporation in the second quarter of this century. You belong to the generation that, in the main, built the modern corporation from the old foundations.

This might have been read as easy generalization if it had not been for a solid piece of Sloan-Durant history a few lines further on in my progress report: "In this connection, I think that the organization document you presented to Durant in 1920 is the foundation document of the story." That is, of "The General Motors Story" and Mr. Sloan's part in it.

This document, entitled "General Motors Corporation/ Organization Study," began: "The object of this study is to suggest an organization for the General Motors Corporation which will definitely place the line of authority throughout its extensive operations as well as to coordinate each branch of its service. . . ." Its twenty-eight pages, replete with organization charts, set forth the future design of the corporation now known in the famous corporate aphorism "decentralization with coordinated control." This document came to us, I believe, from the Du Pont trial record, and early enough in the project that it gave us a lift. Here was a major piece of the design that would give the book its charge.

Not only did the Du Pont company keep good records, but when the Justice Department started suit against them, they invited the FBI to come in and inspect them. Consistent with this, after the Du Ponts had lost in a 4-2 decision, the chief trial lawyer for the Du Ponts, Hugh Cox of the Acheson law firm in Washington, D.C., told me that he had advised Pierre Du Pont at the outset that they would lose in the Supreme Court. Pierre had said that he wanted to fight it anyway, as a matter of honor. The result for our project was a research bonanza as the trial record became available.

The main source of our information would of course have to be General Motors. I had no problem with the General Motors connection; on the contrary, with the independence of the project established, I was glad to get all we could from them in research and in the checking of facts. That would be a large order, with all the areas of knowledge involved in the making and selling of automobiles going back to 1908. On December 15, 1954, Mr. Sloan made a valiant effort to describe the project in the form of a memorandum-letter that was sent to seventeen top officers of the corporation, past and present, including some of the Du Pont group who had crossed over to General Motors; he followed this with a similar memo delivered to the current division and staff heads. In it he described the scope and purpose of the project, and expressed his doubts about depending solely on his own memory to reveal the complete story of General Motors' development. He asked the past and present corporate executives to cooperate "by providing factual information which I can use in the story . . . factual material, opinions, comments, stories, etc. on all phases of the Corporation's activities." He particularly requested that no material be withheld "from the standpoint of policy," but gave assurances that the finished document would be "subject to review on the part of various executives of General Motors, the legal department, and others even outside the corporation, for constructive criticism."

The responses to the memos were lively and factual, together providing an extraordinary picture from the inside of current and past operations of the corporation. During that next full year of 1955 we supplemented these inquiries with direct interviews of selected executives, which were conducted by the three of us: Mr. Sloan, Catharine Stevens, and myself. I had originally thought I could do the job in a year—editing and checking Mr. Sloan's dictated memoir—and at his request had signed up for a year and a half for good measure. Now, with all the information flowing in from those contacts, Mr. Sloan's dictation, some statistical work in the auto industry by a member of our staff, the Du Pont trial records, and the public records of the corporation and automobile industry, we loaded up to such an extent that my progress report to Mr. Sloan of December 6, 1955 noted a big change in the nature of the project: "The need to revise the schedule, as you observed the other day, is due to the fact that the project has grown considerably in length and depth. It has become as much a research and study project as a writing and editing one." The revised plan was for twenty-five chapters, "the equivalent of twenty-five [long] *Fortune* stories," and we extended our agreement through 1956 with a plan to publish in 1957. Around this time, Mr. Sloan, sitting at the head of the conference table where we were working, said: "For the first time, I understand what it is to write a book."

Mr. Sloan's wife, Irene Jackson, died on February 20, 1956, surrounded by doctors and nurses in their Palm Beach house. Catharine Stevens and I, grossly out of place at such an event, happened to be working there at the time. I remember his saying to me in desperation: "John, you just can't help me." True in any case and as it was, nothing could. He tried in every way he could to keep her alive through a long illness and, after a long life together, her death shook him to the core. Mortality had defeated him, and he immediately resigned as chairman of General Motors. I wondered about our project and asked his younger brother Raymond Sloan, who had come to take care of him, what he thought about it. He said that Mr. Sloan had said that as far as the book was concerned: "It's finished." But not everything was. Walter Carpenter, head of the Du Pont company, came to New York and persuaded him not to leave General Motors entirely, but to accept the new title of "Honorary Chairman." This kept his public presence going while he also continued to serve on the Board and committees, a matter of consequence since the government suit against Du Pont was still on, and a changing of the guard at the top of General Motors was due to take place in 1958, just two years off. Albert Bradley had taken Mr. Sloan's place as interim chairman for two years.

Mr. Sloan and his wife had no children. He had a sister and three brothers for whom he had provided, he said, with a trust fund. His brother Raymond, who was seventeen years younger and distinguished and active in the hospital field, appeared closest to him, or at least as close as Mr. Sloan allowed anyone to get other than his wife. His fortune, made almost entirely out of General Motors, went for the most part to the Sloan Foundation, the Sloan-Kettering Medical Center, and the MIT School of Industrial Management, which he referred to collectively and with feeling as "my substance." In his memoir we worked on how he had made his money, not on how he had distributed it. His personal expenditures were relatively modest for his means.

Mr. Sloan was not a very social person when I knew him. His central and occupying interest was business. One might say that business, in essence, was his life. He seemed to play no recreational games. His politics were straight mainline Republican, and even when Barry Goldwater was running far behind in his presidential campaign, Mr. Sloan would urge acquaintances, "Get on the bandwagon." At the same time, in some matters he had an aversion to anything political. The only person I proposed to engage on the project whom he turned down was George Leighton, the former editor of *Harper's*, who was at the time writing for the Republicans in Congress. The apparent party connection, even though with his own preferred party, was for Mr. Sloan a fatal objection. It was a great loss to the project.

In General Motors Mr. Sloan preferred civilian to government business, except in wartime. During World War II and under his direction, the company had made an extraordinary changeover from civilian to war production; his preference for civilian production did not prevent General Motors from becoming a major supplier to the government. In culture and thought, Mr. Sloan was of that school for whom technology was progress, life was work, money was a measure of success, and success the goal. I noticed no religious feeling in him until just after his wife died, when he was visited by religious leaders: Cardinal Spellman came to see him twice, and Raymond said that it was "very, very helpful." Later Billy Graham came to see him; but these visits seemed like the courtesy calls proper in crossover hierarchies. Mr. Sloan's genius, as far as I could see, was in a complex of corporate arrangements and activities; his skill was in the internal strategies of the automobile industry and in the market: He could hold that industry, so to speak, in the palm of his hand. He would take a briefcase home with him and sit next to his wife, holding her hand, though she was unaware of her surroundings in her last years. He did not care for parties, even business parties, if only because he was hard of hearing and the decibel level of noise would rise and inundate his hearing aid, a disability that would increase with age. When we got on a level tone in the privacy of his office we could conduct a normal conversation, but he was bothered by his hearing and eventually I would often write my side of the conversation on cards. At the same time, he would often fail to hear what he did not want to hear, something that could be a game.

Although once a teetotaler, he came to drink a Manhattan with his lunch, which he often took alone in the commercial lunch club of the Rainbow Room. Although a rather institutionalized person, when pressed he had considerable personal wit. A dry outlook lay beneath the adopted persona of self-conscious icon of General Motors. When we taped an interview, as Catharine Stevens said, he would stop and say, "Shut it off," whereupon he would improve immeasurably in what he had to say and the way he said it. Then he might tell a little story. For example, in the presidential election of 1928, he forced John J. Raskob to choose between General Motors and the Democratic Party: Raskob, who came from Du Pont, and with whom Sloan had a rub, was chairman of the General Motors Finance Committee in the 1920s and its chief spokesman. Raskob was also chairman of the Democratic Party. Mr. Sloan explained: "I wanted to sell cars to Republicans, too." He wanted to leave the anecdote out of the book, and, as much as I wanted it in, I could not say it was imperative it be included.

Mr. Sloan told also of a personal encounter with Walter Chrysler one evening in the 1920s at Bradley's, which was a dining and gambling casino in Palm Beach. They had had dinner there together—hard to get into, he said—and after dinner had visited the casino. Chrysler got interested in the crap-game and challenged Bradley to raise the limit to a thousand dollars. Bradley, who was a sport—he was a considerable figure in the breeding and racing of horses—said he would, and he had a special table roped off for Chrysler's sole use. Chrysler rolled and rolled, and lost and lost, until finally he stopped, down $125,000. On their way home together in the car, Walter said to Alfred: "I don't mind the money, I can afford it. What I mind is thinking I could win." They were very different personalities—it is hard to imagine Mr. Sloan in Bradley's—but he liked Chrysler for what he was: a rough and ready automobile producer who had come up from the factory floor.

Mr. Sloan did not engage much in the small talk that others in high places did. At a dinner in his honor in the 1950s, he sat on the dais next to President Eisenhower. Seeing them up there talking together, one might have imagined they were moving big things around. The next day I asked him what they talked about. He said, "Our diets."

Mr. Sloan tended to be loyal to persons around him. His long-time secretary, Miss Kucher, had been with him from the nineteenth century and remained with him at General Motors for her lifetime. She typed with two fingers and spelled according to her likes and was that kind of person. She referred to him as "that man."

So it was with Catharine Stevens. Once they had worked together, early on, he wanted her to continue as his assistant when the project was done. As for me, in the course of the project and difficulties to come his loyalties to friends became a factor. His personal attitude toward me would play an important part in the story of the book.

The project had something useful about it for his state of mind after his wife died. On the occasion of his previous birthday, he had written me a thank-you note for noticing it, saying that at eighty "there is little to look forward to . . . but I have much to look backward on. And, in a way, that's consolation."

He returned to the office after a while—not quite the same person in spirit and confidence. He was interested in how the publishing market would respond to our project. It was time to show something, and so with the materials we had created and gathered I drafted a sample of the proposed book, which Catharine and I completed on May 1, 1956.

The sample, a sizable production of about a hundred manuscript pages, contained an introduction, the first three chapters, and an outline of thirty chapters in all, with a provision for illustrations. It sketched the history of General Motors as the company was loosely put together by William C. Durant beginning in 1908 with Buick and Cadillac, followed in time by Chevrolet, Oakland (predecessor of the Pontiac), Olds (Oldsmobile), Scripps-Booth, and Sheridan (the last two would later be scrapped). There was a period of time after 1910, with which I was much taken, when Durant first lost control of General Motors to bankers, and Charles W. Nash, later of the Nash automobile, became manager of Buick. He hired Walter Chrysler as his works manager and when Nash became president of General Motors, Chrysler became president and general manager of Buick. Meanwhile Durant, now only an outside director of General Motors, backed Louis Chevrolet in a new company making a light car. He then had the Chevrolet company, which he controlled, buy a controlling interest in General Motors. Exercised in 1915, this interest returned to Durant the control of General Motors, the company he had founded seven years before. Nash left to start the Nash Motor Company. To simplify the complexity resulting from Chevrolet swallowing General Motors, Durant merged them into one company, General Motors.

In the course of these corporate musical chairs, Pierre Du Pont bought a little General Motors stock and as a compromise candidate between contending forces—the bankers versus Durant—he was elected chairman of General Motors. Durant wanted capital for expansion and he found it in the Du Pont company, which had more profits from World War I munitions than the family could invest in their own company. John J. Raskob was Pierre Du Pont's mentor and guide in matters of finance, as Charles Kettering came to be in technology—both very good in their fields but with flaws that would endanger the survival of General Motors. With great foresight into the future of the automobile business, Raskob wrote down several good reasons for the Du Pont company to invest in General Motors. Among these reasons, which he numbered, was that together with Durant they could secure joint control of the company and "assume charge and be responsible for the financial operation of the company." His Point Five would later bring big trouble. He wrote: "Our interest in the General Motors Company will undoubtedly secure for us the entire Fabrikoid, Pyralin, paint, and varnish business of those companies, which is a substantial factor." The Du Ponts were persuaded, and in

1917 the Du Pont company made the large investment in General Motors that gave them about a twenty-three percent interest in the company. As proposed by Raskob, the Du Ponts and Durant divided the responsibility for the company, Durant directing operations, with the Du Ponts directing its finances. These roles were represented in the two top committees, Finance and Operations, which have survived in General Motors to this day.

Walter Chrysler left General Motors in 1919, dissatisfied, as Mr. Sloan remembered, with Durant's loose management. In a dramatic finale during the severe recession of 1920, the Du Pont company, assisted by the Morgan Bank, took over General Motors from the unaccountably financially ailing Durant. The negotiation was recorded in detail in a memorandum by Pierre Du Pont. With the company's twenty-three percent and family investing, the Du Ponts now owned about half of all General Motors stock. Durant left—taking his records with him, it seemed, as we could not find them—and the Du Ponts moved in to operate the company.

Mr. Sloan's own beginnings in the industry fit into this complex of interests brought together in General Motors. He had graduated from MIT in 1895, and with the financial assistance of his father he got into the business of making roller bearings, which would become an essential component of the automobile. And so he found himself a supplier to the emerging automobile industry at its beginning. His Hyatt roller bearings went into a number of cars, including those of General Motors and Ford, as these companies grew in the teens. In 1916 Durant, who had recaptured General Motors the year before, was out looking over the automobile and accessories fields and created a new company, United Motors, into which he brought a half-dozen producers of bearings, electrical equipment, rims, and such. Mr. Sloan was interested in part because, with half of his business going to Ford and the prospect of future obsolescence of his product, he felt vulnerable. He took Hyatt into United Motors in 1916 and, as its president and chief operating officer, added to it the producers of the Klaxon horn and other parts and accessories. Two years later Durant took United Motors into General Motors and Mr. Sloan went with it.

At General Motors, Mr. Sloan took it upon himself to think about how to make this collection of cars and car components work as an internally coordinated entity. Hence his "Organization Study," which he wrote for Durant and, after Durant's fall, had ready for the new Du Pont control and administration of General Motors. During the 1919–1920 economic crisis he nearly resigned to become a management consultant, but when Pierre Du Pont took over in 1920 and formed a top executive committee of four, three of whom were from the Du Pont company, he got Mr. Sloan to join them. Of the four, only Mr. Sloan had operating experience in the automobile industry.

In the sample manuscript we drafted in 1956, we also sketched the substance of Mr. Sloan's "Organization Study" of 1919–1920, describing the structure of a great integrated organization whose market strategy would come to be expressed as "a car for every purse and purpose." We took the story up to Pierre Du Pont's resignation from operations in 1923 in favor of Mr. Sloan, when he arranged Mr. Sloan's election as president and chief executive of General Motors. The sample thus contained the nucleus of the book with the characters, themes, essential elements, and direction lines in place.

The sample was completed and a hundred copies made and ready to go out on May 1, 1956. The copy I still have is number seventy-seven. We sent it out for comment and criticism to

many people, including the executives we had previously con-
tacted, and others outside the General Motors/Du Pont area. I
gave a copy to Hedley Donovan, managing editor of *Fortune*,
and a copy went to Henry R. ("Harry") Luce, editor-in-chief
of Time Inc. For our approach to book publishers, I introduced
Mr. Sloan to Harold Matson, one of the leading literary agents
in New York. We met in Mr. Sloan's office, Mr. Sloan behind
his desk, a seating that Matson himself preferred when negotiating with publishers.

Mr. Sloan said: "Mr. Matson, I don't know your business.
Who do you represent?" Mr. Matson replied: "I represent you,
Mr. Sloan. The publisher is the enemy." Mr. Sloan gave his
signal smile of appreciation, and Mr. Matson was our agent.
He, of course, knew how to cooperate with publishers when
the time came.

Matson was known for putting a prospective book out for
bids when he thought there was a strong market for it, common
procedure nowadays but bold at the time. Any bid could be
overbid: It was an auction. Matson offered the Sloan book to
several book publishers in this manner.

The publishing market responded as well as one could wish.
The leading magazine publisher, Henry R. Luce, wrote to Mr.
Sloan on June 14 that it gave him "a real thrill to have this
manuscript in my hands. . . . I have long thought that it was
important that your creative experience in business organization should be definitively recorded. We [*sic*] started out with
the idea that you should write an article summarizing some of
your conclusions. A full-length book is of course something of
a quite different nature. The book in itself is a much more important project and, as I said, I am delighted that you are engaged in a work of this magnitude. When the book is finished

we will then have the pleasurable task of working out the problem of its partial presentation in *Fortune*."

Hedley Donovan also wrote to Mr. Sloan on June 7:

John McDonald has shown me the Introduction and first three chapters of "The General Motors Story." You certainly whet my appetite for more.

I found the Introduction especially interesting and would have no difficulty in visualizing it as a *Fortune* article pretty much as it stands. From the promise of what I have seen and from the scope of the outline of the book as a whole, I have no doubt that there are the makings of an interesting and important *Fortune* series here—i.e., at least three or four articles, though naturally I'm hoping for more.

Meanwhile, for whatever my opinion may be worth, I wanted you to know that I was much impressed with the material I saw. I realize, of course, that this represents only a small part of the work that has been done so far. I know nothing about the book business and less about the magazine business than I would like to, but I believe you are well into a very successful project which, both as a book and in its magazine by-products, is going to be a valuable contribution to the understanding of American enterprise.

Mr. Sloan was pleased with the reception at Time Inc., but became apprehensive when returns from the auction came in. The book publishers responded to Matson in a range of offers. At the low end Simon and Schuster wanted first a new editor (and to get rid of me) and Harcourt Brace wanted a more popular approach; they would bid for another, different book. Harper made a strong bid but Doubleday made a stronger one. Matson had not, at first, included Doubleday in the auction, but when Doubleday's distinguished young editor Jason Epstein heard of it, he got Doubleday to make the preemptive bid:

July 18, 1956
Dear Hal:
We here at Doubleday are tremendously excited about the sample material for Alfred P. Sloan's "The Story of General Motors."

Ten or twelve of us have now read this material and we have prepared a statement of our publishing plans which I am enclosing in
triplicate.

We would like to offer a royalty of fifteen percent (15%) and an
advance or guarantee of $50,000. dollars against the earnings of this
book under contract. It is understood that this guarantee is against
book rights only (including book club and reprint) in the United States,
Canada, Philippine Islands and open markets.

Sincerely yours,
LeBaron R. Barker, Jr.
Executive Editor

Doubleday's bid was accompanied by a description of a substantial publishing program, at least as costly as their advance
offer; and their editors' observation on the quality of the
project:

Should the remaining chapters of Mr. Sloan's book maintain the quality of the three sample chapters, as we assume they will, the result will
be a document in American social and economic history as significant
in its own [way] as was "The Education of Henry Adams" in American
cultural history. . . . "The General Motors Story" is likely therefore
to be neither a company history nor a business book in the usual sense
but a major item in our national record. Should Doubleday and Company become Mr. Sloan's publishers our presentation of this book
would begin on this assumption. . . .

Their hopes may be read as a bit extravagant. Mr. Sloan's
fear was that we could be misleading the publishers on future
"drama"; that the book could never live up to the excitement
of the sample with its climax in the fall of Durant and the takeover by the Du Ponts. This, he thought, might account for the
conditional response of Simon and Schuster and Harcourt
Brace. Mr. Sloan, Catharine Stevens, and I met on July 13
to discuss the first reports on Matson's auction, including
Doubleday's bid. Part of the conversation went as follows
(from a transcript):

*John:*   Simon and Schuster had not originally bid, and they asked for the right to bid. Max Schuster telephoned [Matson] and said he knew you. He doesn't want to submit a formal bid in writing. He wants to have a meeting with you. I told Mr. Matson that I would recommend it, but that I would disapprove.

[Mr. Sloan agrees with John that he should not meet with Simon and Schuster. He says that Mr. Matson is the agent who was handling the matter and that it was being done through written bids.]

*Mr. Sloan:*   One thing—I don't want to keep emphasizing this—but all my life I have tried to deal equitably with people and not hold anything back on them. I feel very keenly that whomever we decide to give the job to, and perhaps discuss this with Mr. Matson before, I feel that no matter how smart we are and no matter how much effort we put into it, that the nature of the chapters cannot be as dynamic as the first three chapters. It's just not in the picture. The rest of the chapters are going to be tremendously interesting, I'm sure, and I think that they will have a big demand from businessmen who want to know about it and from the standpoint of the *Saturday Evening Post* and *Colliers,* or, perhaps, *Life* readers, and I think that [this doubt about future drama] ought to be put before the publisher.

*John:*   You're getting ahead of me. You raised the question and I took it up with Mr. Matson. I told him that I thought that the other chapters would be somewhat different.

*Mr. Sloan:*   More prosaic.

*John:*   I don't use the same words you do, because I have a way to handle it. The subject matter is different. We don't have another Durant blow-up. That's a drama.

*Mr. Sloan:*    And you don't have another introduction where you can lay down thinking, et cetera.

*John:*    Mr. Sloan, there can only be one introduction to any book. [Really! Could I have said that? I have published books with more than one.]

[Mr. Sloan laughs.]

*John:*    I'm not going to do anything about that. But business is interesting generally. It's true we don't have a Durant blow-up . . . but we do have a lot of things. Six years later GM passes Ford and Ford shuts down; your forcing Raskob to resign; the Depression after seven years of up-swinging and a suddenly saturated automobile market and depression on top of it; then it goes on until we get into the war, and then the war crisis.

You know what a *Fortune* article is like. It has structure, a certain aesthetic of industrial drama. Let me tell you about this book. There are thirty chapters. Each is the equivalent of one *Fortune* story, but they happen to be related. In writing a *Fortune* story, you have just as many problems of drama, et cetera. Each chapter in this book has the same problem. Each has to be organized separately. Each sentence has to be hooked to the whole. . . .

[I had spoken to Mr. Matson and asked him whether he thought the publishers could misunderstand the rest of the book. Mr. Matson said: "I don't see how the publishers could misunderstand."]

You may create more misunderstanding if you raise this question with the publisher. May I ask you to do this: You use broadly the term "dramatic." You say the rest of the book is not going to be as dramatic as the first three chapters. If you don't mind, I'd like to become more precise and say: The remainder of the book doesn't have the same type of dramatic subject matter. You must say subject matter. We are going to treat this book on the same high level as the beginning.

*Mr. Sloan:*    Let's put this book back on the stove.

We all met with Matson, who made a detailed analysis of the bidding, concluding that Doubleday's was by far the best. Mr. Sloan continued to be anxious about our ability to measure up to Doubleday's expectations in terms of "dramatic interest." In an exchange between them Matson persuaded Mr. Sloan that Doubleday knew what it was doing and Mr. Sloan finally said: "You draw up a formal contract between me and Doubleday. . . ."

On August 20, about a month after he had told Matson to draw up a contract and Matson had gone ahead with it to Doubleday, Mr. Sloan wrote me a letter in legalistic style saying that he had talked with his lawyer Moore and that he would not sign a publishing agreement with Doubleday. I suppose Mr. Sloan should be considered dauntless within limits to have undertaken his business memoir with a commitment to sound history in the face of a new Justice Department investigation of General Motors as well as the ongoing Du Pont–General Motors suit— the latter going before the Supreme Court. And I suppose I should not have been surprised when he reneged on the Doubleday contract. There followed over the next several weeks an acrimonious exchange between Mr. Sloan and me in letters and meetings, Mr. Sloan citing his right to cancel, I acknowledging that right but citing the negative consequences to me if he should cancel the book in the future. In this standoff we came close to splitting, Mr. Sloan stating that if I "washed out" he would "wash out" the project. His lawyer, Moore, who had initially proposed a publishing contract, had reversed himself and now opposed it, embarrassing Matson. Mr. Sloan said that Moore felt Mr. Sloan would never get the book past General Motors, but Mr. Sloan told me that he did not agree with that. We reached a compromise in which Doubleday would get the book on the same terms in which they had bid, with a guarantee but no advance payment and no delivery date. And I understood that if publication did not take place, Mr. Sloan would in some way protect me from the consequences.

I was inclined to go along with such a loose arrangement because of Mr. Sloan's personal assurances. Furthermore, I had reason to doubt that Moore's information was as good as Mr. Sloan's; Moore's was coming from Cravath, and Mr. Sloan's from the group he "consulted," that is, sounded out, on the Finance Committee, which was the senior committee of the corporation. This committee was not at the moment quite as powerful as Mr. Sloan thought it should be, owing to the fact that the post of chief executive of the corporation had been vested in the president rather than the chairman. Judging by his responses to our requests, the then-president and chief executive of General Motors, Harlow Curtice, took no evident interest in the book. He was scheduled for mandatory retirement at age sixty-five, in 1958, when if all went well for him—which was not at all certain—he would become chairman. If not Curtice, in Detroit, the next chairman would likely be Frederic Donner, from the financial side in New York. As it seemed that the book would be completed before these and other changes at the top took place, there did not seem to be anyone who would want to overrule Mr. Sloan. Henry Hogan, the inside chief counsel, attended Finance Committee meetings but was not a member; his views would be influential but not decisive. Mr. Sloan wanted the approval of "General Motors," but the situation in General Motors was not monolithic. So the issue rested.

To survive, the project had to get through a little crisis in its management, which came as a surprise during the ordinary course of developments. In his reply to Luce of July 3, 1956, Mr. Sloan wrote: "As you might appreciate, the story covers a period of thirty to forty years and presents a great many circumstances which are not in the record and have to be carefully checked and so many [persons] have passed out in the meantime that presents real difficulty."

The "difficulty" here was how to cope with the large quantity of information required to do what the sample said we would do: how the three of us, he and Catharine and I, were to proceed with a project of such magnitude. The answer, of course, dictated by particular needs, added up to a major expansion of the project, its office staff, researchers, writers, editors, consultants, and such. The sample, where it left off historically in the early twenties, implied a new frontier of research.

We had preferred primary sources all along, but no particular decision along this line had more consequences in story and trouble than the one we made in 1956 to have Mr. Sloan open General Motors' files, especially forward from 1918, the year he had entered the corporation. We had different expectations, as noted earlier, of the story value of what we might find in the files, Mr. Sloan being pessimistic about there being anything very exciting there, I believing that there had to be something interesting behind such wrenching external events as the change of position with Ford at the top of the automobile market in the twenties. This meant following the paper trail at General Motors, of everything from minutes of the board of directors and major permanent and special committees to thoughts, discussions, and developments in organization, finance, and line and staff operations, strategies of the car market, and all such documents, in search of material for our study and the refreshment of Mr. Sloan's memory, as well as to provide a check on his memory. Despite the difference in our expectations we agreed on the main thing: to open the files. And with that decided we took up the effect this would have on our project.

I wanted a long-term research assistant, preferably a trained academic historian, to work with us and to check on work we had done. Mr. Sloan agreed, and I was to engage such a person.

But then Mr. Sloan went off the track.

Having learned of a prospective candidate from a dean at MIT who had read the sample, Mr. Sloan met with him and, before I knew what happened, engaged him to join the project for a year. I strenuously objected to the candidate as unsuitable and to the procedure as unworkable. At lunch with me after his meeting with Mr. Sloan, the engaged candidate seemed to believe that he would be responsible for the "noneditorial" side of the project, a sort of overseer rather than the worker we needed. Mr. Sloan's blunder, as I saw it, inspired me to write him a long, rather sharp memorandum on project management, with due reference to decentralization, as the project was moving into its big expansion.

In my memo, dated July 29, 1956, I called into question not only the candidate's qualifications, but also Mr. Sloan's actions in meeting the man independently and apparently hiring him without consulting me. I pointed out the danger to the project of "the separation of function and responsibility on the project. [Because] . . . the responsibility for the book cannot effectively be divided any further than it has been from the beginning, that is between you and me." Summarizing the previous administrative arrangements, which had worked well, I asked Mr. Sloan to reconsider his decision and (in a supplementary note the following day) to do so immediately, "before [the candidate] takes an irrevocable step regarding his present university commitment," or at the least to clear up any misapprehension the candidate might have had regarding the nature of the job.

In this confrontation with Mr. Sloan, loading up on requirements and rules of an expanding project was rewarded not only by his prompt disengagement of the wrong candidate but also by the engagement of the right one. Resuming the search at universities, I went back to Morris Adelman at MIT, this time for a suggestion. He named a prospect, Alfred D. Chandler, a young teacher and scholar in the field of American industrial history, still years away from his Pulitzer prizes and other distinctions to come. Catharine and I looked into Chandler's work, met him, and found him to be a promising and willing candidate as our research assistant and consultant. That his middle initial "D." stood for Du Pont was no problem. Unconscious biases perhaps could occur, but his integrity as a research scholar was clear and solid, and if his being a "cousin" in the clan eased his way when we sent him into General Motors, that would be fine, although with Mr. Sloan requesting our access to the files it would be unnecessary. The principal assignment we had in mind for him was to review and report to us on General Motors files, where he was to be on the lookout particularly for materials written or inspired by Mr. Sloan himself during his first ten turbulent and most creative years at General Motors—the quality of which we were familiar with from Mr. Sloan's "Organization Study" of 1919–1920. I recommended Chandler to Mr. Sloan as a candidate so well suited to the task—he had the intelligence, energy, and motivation to work well at both high and low levels of research—that we need look no further; I arranged for them to meet and Mr. Sloan confirmed his engagement. In view of the tensions between Mr. Sloan and me, I was glad, after this was done, to find him pleased by the switch from his candidate to mine. It brought to the expanding book project the rule of management encapsulated in his aphorism: "decentralization with coordinated control."

It's worth mentioning here, I think, that in addition to the fifteen or so of Mr. Sloan's old associates who offered their memories and observations from their rare knowledge of the subject, we enlisted a remarkable team of professionals— altogether twenty-some persons at one time or another. Expansion also gave Catharine Stevens the opportunity to exercise more of her capabilities for office and project management. She was now a lieutenant commander in the Naval Reserve, a specialist in office management. According to a note I made of a meeting at the time (dated September 20, 1956), "Mr. Sloan said that he appreciated the extraordinary work that Miss Stevens performed on the project and thought she was the best person in her kind of work that he had ever met, and he thought she was entitled to a share of ownership in the project"—which he then awarded her out of his share, eventually thirty percent of the whole. She became the focal point and organizer of the research projects, in charge of outside contacts—including that with the keeper of General Motors' files—fact-checker, critic of manuscripts, and keeper of our files, with a separate set for each of us. And as she said, "I felt at home with Mr. Sloan all the time." When near-splitting tensions occurred between Mr. Sloan and me her presence kept the project together.

**September 1956–February 1959**

When this new activity, actual and forecast, had its inevitable manifestation in a budget Catharine and I drew up, Mr. Sloan backed off again. "Too big," he said. Cutting back would of course mean engaging less paid assistance in research and drafting, altering both the envisioned quality of the book and its time scale; but it was his money. I tried a ploy. I went to see his protégé, then General Motors' interim chairman, Albert Bradley, whose judgment he respected, showed him the budget, and asked what he thought of it. He looked it over and said it looked okay to him. That's all I wanted, but Bradley, a person of some wit, added, "I'll pay it." "Contrary to our policy," I said. When I quoted Bradley to Mr. Sloan, all he heard was that General Motors was willing to pay. "No, no!" he cried, and approved the budget. With all our friction in the past and the work moving harmoniously, Mr. Sloan said, one day: "I'd rather be doing this than anything."

With these arrangements, I said one more year should do it. Always one more. It took two. I have no intention of making here even a sketch of Mr. Sloan's book, but a couple of episodes from his past are needed for their bearing on what eventually happened to the book and my connection with it. These involved the "copper-cooled" engine and the 1921 Product Policy, both described below.

Alfred Chandler's densely packed reports on the paper trail at General Motors, written by request in the first person, began to come in during March, 1957. We selected original documents of major interest for study and publication. These were pristine documents kept unpruned over four decades. Mr. Sloan and the Du Pont group in General Motors were remarkably articulate businessmen, spelling out what they wanted to do and what they did in the management of General Motors after they took over its operations from Durant. Reading the documents is like going to school in management, rich material for Mr. Sloan's memoir, as a number of them had been written by him or drafted with his supervision during the most creative period of his business life.

Mr. Sloan was often surprised and of course pleased to read what he had written or participated in formulating so long ago. His worry was soon dispelled that there would be a lack of drama in General Motors of the 1920s after the spectacular departure of its founder Durant in 1920. Multiple sets of the General Motors documents revealed at least as much drama, more in weight, in the first three years of the Du Pont–Sloan administration. As noted, the drama of Durant was his personal loss of control of General Motors in a morass of stock-market maneuvers during the rapid decline of the stock market, in particular the General Motors stock in the economic slump of 1920, as Durant and Morgan ran what appeared to be intolerably competing syndicates presumably supporting General Motors stock while in a few months it lost about seventy-five percent of its market value. Questions are still asked about a conflict between Morgan and Durant, but there is no question that Durant got himself under water in the stock market and had to sell his controlling interest in General Motors to the only buyers at hand: the Du Ponts, assisted by the Morgans. It was one of the great business dramas, and there was enough substance there to suggest that there would have been a General Motors with or without Durant.

As Chandler's research made clear, Pierre Du Pont, on taking charge of General Motors as chairman, president, and chief executive of the corporation and general manager of Chevrolet, working diligently but with no operating experience in the automobile business and no one to overrule him, gambled the existence of General Motors on the success of a new air-cooled engine—called "copper-cooled" for its copper fins brazed or welded to the engine walls—developed by his research chief, Charles Kettering. Du Pont ordered the engine to be installed in one line of General Motors cars after another from 1921 to

1923. The engine failed. That General Motors didn't fail with it was owing largely to resistance on the part of automobile executives in line operations led by Mr. Sloan, who quietly and out of sight, as it were, kept Chevrolet alive with the water-cooled engine, ready for the return of a strong automobile market in 1923. As we were going over this matter one day, Mr. Sloan turned to Catharine and me and said, "I was really independent, wasn't I?" As Chandler saw the moral of the copper-cooled story, they, the Du Pont–Sloan management together, "took a calculated business risk and lost." We disagreed with Chandler's judgment; in the documents of the time Pierre Du Pont's copper-cooled engine policy reads less like a calculation than like Pierre's blind faith in Kettering. In July 1921, Kettering said of his new engine, "It is the greatest thing that has ever been produced in the automobile world." That fall Pierre Du Pont wrote to Kettering: "Now that we are at the point of planning production of the new cars I am beginning to feel like a small boy when the long expected circus posters begin to appear on the fences, and to wonder how each part of the circus is to appear and what act I will like best." Pierre's heady optimism was not shared by Mr. Sloan, GM engineers, or the line executives—heads of the car divisions—who were ordered by Pierre to produce cars with Kettering's experimental and soon-to-fail engine.

It was thus more interesting than the win-one, lose-one risks customarily taken by chief executives. As Mr. Sloan saw it, his memory revived by the documents, it was not necessary to try to gain a big edge in technology. If you had a good car, a good market strategy would suffice—not a prescription to lag in technology but in this instance to avoid committing the line divisions to an untried engine without a backup. One of the chief engineers in General Motors at the time, Ormond E. Hunt, who at the time was called in to appraise the new engine, confirmed Mr. Sloan's view of it in a long letter dated January 21, 1959, which included a list of detailed comments.

The records of the copper-cooled engine episode more than satisfied Mr. Sloan's doubts about drama. And although the records had been buried in General Motors files and forgotten since the early twenties, on review the incident appeared to have had some impact on Mr. Sloan's thoughts about and practice of line and staff management in General Motors all along— which came as a surprise when it surfaced in his book.

Most remarkable and strategically potent, however, was the product policy devised by Mr. Sloan's automobile group and set down in writing on May 4, 1921, under the title "Future Manufacturing Lines of General Motors Corporation." Among the members of the advisory committee in General Motors who drafted and signed the product policy were major pioneers of the automobile industry in the United States: Charles Stewart Mott of Flint, Michigan, supplier of axles (rear ones, taking Hyatt bearings); Norval A. Hawkins, formerly chief of sales at Ford; and Charles Kettering, noted for his early work on the self-starter and now, with the copper-cooled engine, head of General Motors' research. In a policy statement to the corporation in 1925, Mr. Sloan included a copy of the 1921 Product Policy, which was the copy that survived for us. It put a charge into the new General Motors, likewise into our book, so much so, as we shall see, that it figured in the silencing of the book. Mr. Sloan was still proud of the policy statement, business-wise, when we read it in 1957.

I quote from it here, as it began with the most general concept of the business and went into detail on what would come to be the General Motors concept of the business:

It has been assumed to start with that the General Motors Corporation is today just commencing business with a capital of approximately $600,000,000 and that preliminary decisions are being made regarding the lines to be manufactured. Since such is not the case in fact, this report should be construed as a recommendation of policy standards toward which the Corporation should work. The aim of the committee has been to chart the "true, best course" for the future operations of the Corporation, recognizing that present actual conditions necessitate sailing off the recommended course temporarily. Before considering the subject of particular products it is advisable to outline the controlling purposes that presumably underlie the organization and proposed operations of the Corporation. That is, the *whole picture* should first be clearly drawn in order that the present particular subject may be considered, not just alone, but in its essential relations to the chief objectives of the General Motors Corporation.

It is to be presumed that the first purpose in making a capital investment is the establishment of a business that will both pay satisfactory dividends and preserve and increase the capital value. The primary object of the General Motors Corporation, therefore, is to make *money*, not just to make motor cars.

*How* is it proposed to earn satisfactory dividends on the investment? And how does the earning purpose of the General Motors Corporation *differ* from the business objectives of other manufacturers of automobile vehicles?

A monopoly is not planned. It is recognized that there will always be competing cars. But it is believed that by "covering the market for *all* grades of automobiles that can be produced and sold in large quantities" the Corporation will be able to secure many advantages over manufacturers of but one or two grades; even if General Motors cars in the respective grades are no better than the best competing automobiles of the same grade. . . .

[A]s soon as practicable the following grades shall constitute the entire line of cars,

(a)  $450.00 – $600.00
(b)  $600.00 – $900.00
(c)  $900.00 – $1200.00
(d)  $1200.00 – $1700.00
(e)  $1700.00 – $2500.00
(f)  $2500.00 – $3500.00

It is recognized that there will always be a considerable market for cars priced above $3500.00, but the demand for any one type will be limited to such a number as would not permit of "quantity" production. These might almost be called custom-built cars, and it is not recommended that the General Motors Corporation attempt to cover that field.

The field of cars of the first grade is now practically monopolized by the Ford. At present it is being invaded by Chevrolet. It is not recommended that the General Motors Corporation attempt to build and sell a car of the Ford grade, as the Ford sells at the lowest price within the first grade. Instead it is recommended that the General Motors Corporation market a car much better than the Ford, with a view to selling it at or near the top price in the first grade. It is not proposed to compete with the Ford grade, but to produce a car that will be so superior to the Ford, yet so near the Ford price, that demand will be drawn from the Ford grade and lifted to the slightly higher price in preference to putting up with the Ford deficiencies.

It is believed that the converse of this effect will be produced when the new General Motors first grade car, selling at approximately $600.00, is compared with cars of competitors in the next highest grade, selling at $750.00 or slightly below. Even though the new General Motors (a) grade car may not be quite as good as competing cars selling at approximately $750.00, it should be so near the grade of competing cars selling at the middle of the second price range, that prospective buyers will prefer to save $150.00 and to yield the comparatively slight preference they might have for the competing car if the prices were nearly equal . . .

In general it should be noted that the price steps recommended by the Committee leave no wide gaps in the line anywhere. Yet they are so planned as to limit the number of cars necessary to produce the smallest possible number sufficient to cover the entire field range for quality production. Unless the number of models is so limited, and unless it is planned that each model will cover its own grade and also overlap into the grades above and below its price, as above outlined on the preceding pages of this report, a large volume cannot be secured for each car. This large volume is necessary to gain the advantages of quantity production counted on as a most important factor in earning a position of pre-eminence in all the grade fields.

There should be absolutely no duplication within the Corporation of any car planned to cover a particular grade field, since a sufficient selection of models will be offered by the overlapping sales scopes of each model, above and below the limits of its planned price range. All competition within the Corporation itself should be eliminated.

It is recognized that the future of the Corporation and its earning power depend on its ability to design and produce automobiles of maximum utility value and attractiveness of appearance, in such quantities and by such coordinated methods of efficiency as will result in a minimum cost for the models required to supply all the markets of greatest demand for automobiles. . . .

The core of the policy, as we wrote in *My Years with General Motors,* lay "in its concept of mass producing a line of cars graded upward in quality and price. This principle supplied the first element in differentiating the General Motors concept from the old Ford Model T concept of the market." (The term "price" was later changed to "chassis cost at 'standard volume.'") And it was a strategy for approaching the market as a whole that would in the future by virtue of its interactive power be adopted by Ford and Chrysler.

A clear example during these years of the way the concept of the interaction between price levels worked was the lower and upper sides of the Chevrolet market. On the lower, as noted, was the top side of the Ford market, which was being invaded by Chevrolet. Then in 1924 and 1925, a price gap— a space with no GM car—appeared on the upper side of the Chevrolet range. Into that gap came a new model car from Hudson Motors, the Essex Coach, which threatened the top side of the Chevrolet market as Chevrolet threatened the top of the Ford market. Mr. Sloan then had General Motors design a car for the gap that would share with Chevrolet in coordinated economies of manufacturing. That strategically designed car was the Pontiac. With the phasing out of the Oakland and scrapping of the Scripps-Booth and Sheridan, the basic five car lines of General Motors were settled as Chevrolet, Pontiac,

Olds, Buick, and Cadillac, designed and operated in accordance with the principles of the Product Policy of 1921.

This was pretty exciting stuff for us, and was to be published for the first time in our book. Mr. Sloan and I gave an entire chapter, chapter 4, to the Product Policy and planned to put the full document in an appendix.

We had not attempted to deal with the government's suit beginning in 1949 against the presence of the Du Ponts in General Motors—an ongoing litigation when we started the book. But then the Du Ponts, after having their case upheld in lower court, lost 4–2 in the Supreme Court on June 3, 1957. They were held in violation of the Clayton Act owing to the fact that as a supplier, the Du Pont company got a lot of the paint business of General Motors, in which they had a controlling stock interest. There was further litigation afterward over aspects of the divorce of Du Pont from General Motors, but the clear result was that the Du Ponts were forced to leave General Motors, and now that the case was essentially over Mr. Sloan wanted to comment on it briefly as he interpreted it in our book. His draft based much of the case against Du Pont on Raskob's 1917 report recommending the Du Pont investment in General Motors, particularly Point Five, which said that with the investors sharing control with Durant they would get General Motors' paint and other business.

General Motors' chief counsel, Henry Hogan, took a different view. In line with our custom when there was disagreement over a text, I met Hogan to discuss the Du Pont footnote. I write here from a record of our conversation: He said that Point Five did not make the government's case but that it did give the antitrust division prosecutors something in writing to show the Attorney General to get the OK to sue. The case against Du Pont, Hogan said, really was that Du Pont bought into GM to get control, and with control they could force officers and directors to buy and give Du Pont a monopoly on Du Pont products. The rest is evidence to support this case, which the Du Ponts won against the government contention in the lower court and lost in the Supreme Court. Hogan thought, as he put it, that Mr. Sloan liked the Point Five issue because "it put the bee on Du Pont's back instead of anything that General Motors did."

Hogan said, "The Du Ponts believe that if they make something it is the most wonderful thing in the world and the price they are charging is the best price they can give you, and on service, they think they give the best service possible. They wonder why you don't give them business. They believe in reciprocity. We don't believe in it at GM. Reciprocity is no good. We have resisted it in the railroads, keeping it out of the diesel locomotive business."

He also explained to me that Du Pont was an "archive" company—I learned the expression from him—whereas General Motors was not. "We don't believe in archives," he said. I knew there was a physical difference in their record-keeping, the Du Ponts orderly, General Motors pretty casual, but I hadn't realized that this was a manifestation of a deeper policy. "GM's way, you lose some good things and get rid of some bad. The Du Ponts," he said, "worked like this: They would have a meeting here one day and that night dictate a memorandum on it so that you would know what they did." When the government started its suit, he said, the Du Ponts invited the FBI in to look over their records. General Motors would not do that. Hogan agreed to send me something in writing, a page or so, on the legalities of the case for use in our next draft on the subject.

In May 1958, Mr. Sloan led the way in effecting a major change in the structure of committees at the top of General

Motors. The president and outgoing chief executive, Harlow Curtice, normally would have been expected to become chairman, but that post along with the post of chief executive went now to Frederic Donner, from the financial staff. Harlow Curtice had upset Mr. Sloan by his method of conducting a price war between Chevrolet and Ford, in 1955. Ford, it appears, started it and Curtice responded by shunting cars around from regular franchise dealers to discount lots. The dealers protested to Mr. Sloan, but when he took the issue to the Finance Committee they were unable to persuade Curtice and lacked the power to instruct him. Curtice, who was then president, chief executive, and head of the Operations Committee, went ahead as he chose. This led Mr. Sloan to rethink the power hierarchy in General Motors and to his decision to bring the power back from Detroit and from Operations to Finance. He accomplished this by restoring the Finance Committee to its former dominance. Its chairman was made chief executive. Curtice was denied his expected election to chairman. Donner's election as chairman and chief executive thereby also started a new line of succession. These changes had no direct bearing on the book, but my impression is that had we finished Mr. Sloan's book while there was still uncertainty about the new appointments, there wouldn't have been anyone around who would have wanted to get in its way.

As it was, in November 1958 we finished the book, the first complete draft, about eight hundred pages of manuscript in two volumes, the narrative occupying the first, followed by the set of discrete subjects; and we promised an appendix of documents from the 1920s. It was bound in twenty-five copies, and sent out to Doubleday, to *Fortune*/Time Inc., to our standing list of commentators in the General Motors/Du Pont areas, to Mr. Sloan's associates both past and present, and to consultants. From these quarters we received a flood of favorable responses in both generalization and detail, and a renewal of strong interest from book and magazine publishers. Despite our critical treatment of Pierre Du Pont's administration of General Motors in the early 1920s, Walter Carpenter wrote that the book had "the eloquence of facts" and enclosed the opinion of Du Pont's chief counsel—no objections. No objections from anywhere.

## 1959–1960

On January 15, 1959, Mr. Sloan, Catharine Stevens, and I met in Mr. Sloan's office with Douglas Black, president of Doubleday, Kenneth McCormick, its editor-in-chief, and John Sargent, its secretary, to revive the agreement of 1956 and arrange for the publication of the book at the top of their list in 1959. The minutes show Mr. Sloan leading off with a question:

*Mr. Sloan:*   Do we have a merchandisable product?

*Mr. Black:*   Yes, very much so.

*Mr. McCormick:*   We are very keen about this book.

*Mr. Black:*   We are all convinced that the serious reader of books will look on it not only as a story of General Motors, or an important business book, but also as a readable contemporary history.

*Mr. Sloan:*   . . . Perhaps we will be criticized for having too much documentation. . . . We had to dig into the records. I think the documentation is important, but from your point of view it may not be.

*Mr. Black:*   We don't feel that the documentation gets in the way. . . . It is very clear to us that the documents serve to refresh your recollection. It is clear that you are not drawing only on your very good memory but are drawing also on the original documents and reporting on them.

*Mr. Sloan:*   Are you prepared to publish this book?

*Mr. Black:*   We are indeed, sir.

*Mr. Sloan:*   Then the logical thing is to have a contract. . . . I would like to tell Mr. Moore to get together with your people [and Mr. Matson] and work out a contract. He has to do it because it involves my tax position. He will work out the contract. Will that be fair?

*Mr. Black:*   That will be fine. We have talked to Mr. Matson.

*[Decision:*   Mr. Moore will get together with Mr. Black and Mr. Matson to work out the contract.

*Publication Date:*   The publication date is discussed. Mr. Black says that October 1959 would be the publication date. Next, deadlines are discussed in order to meet this publication date.]

*Mr. Black:*   The manuscript is needed as soon as possible. It is in very good shape. We would need to have the complete manuscript by April first to make the October publishing date.

*Mr. Sloan:*   Part I is pretty well finished. We have sent it to quite a few people. . . . Would it help if we released part I before part II?

*Mr. Black:*   Yes.

*Mr. Sloan:*   Suppose we give you part I by the first of March . . . then would it be OK if we gave you part II by the first of May?

[The answer was no—they would have to have part II by April first in order to publish in October.]

*Mr. Black:*   Part I is a book that the man in the street will want and get and read. Part II will undoubtedly add a great deal. Are they separable? That raises another question re part II. Should these volumes be published together simultaneously both in one volume? It is our feeling that part I is the main part of the story. . . .

*Mr. Sloan:*   Let's talk about that. In the first place, I feel it is unwise to have a book too big and too heavy.

*Mr. Black:*   We brought some samples.

[He shows Mr. Sloan two books.]

*Mr. Sloan:*   I think two volumes of that size [of *New Found World*] would be very nice. If it is too big, people can't carry it with them. . . . What would be the selling price at retail?

*Mr. Black:*   We have done all the estimating we can. We had thought of $7.00 for one and if we did the two together, it couldn't be less than $10.00.

*Mr. Sloan:*   I was thinking of $10.00 myself. If we had two volumes would we publish them at the same time?

*Mr. Black:*   We had thought that it might be desirable to publish one in the fall and another in the spring, but it would be discussed when we have full information on the two volumes.

*Mr. Sloan:*   Mr. Moore had seen part I and he is very enthusiastic about it. He sent it out to Harry Luce who is there in Arizona. . . . He [Mr. Moore] is anxious that if there is any delay on part II to get part I out as soon as we could. I think you have to consider that the two parts are quite different. Part I is more history, more philosophy. . . . When we get to part II we deal with the research activities, how we produce a new car, etc. I think we can have the manuscript to you by April first. . . . Part I is now about 90,000 words, or 336 pages, without the preface, index, illustrations, footnotes, documents, etc. Altogether it will probably run to 125,000 words roughly. Part II is now about 110,000 words without an introduction or index;

with those and revisions it will probably run about 125,000 words. The same as part I. . . .

*Mr. Black:* How many pages would the documents cover roughly?

*Mr. McDonald:* About another 10,000 or 15,000 words, plus a few thousand more words for preface, footnotes and the like, so that actually both volumes will come to about the same size.

*Mr. Sloan:* We'll give you the completed manuscript April first. . . . Part I will be finished before that. . . . I think we can do it by the middle of March. That will enable us to get it published in September or October.

*Mr. Black:* October.

*Mr. Sloan:* We'll decide later whether we'll have one volume or two volumes. . . . *Fortune* magazine is interested in the story. If they should come out with a series would it help the book?

*Mr. Black:* It would help the book.

[The Doubleday men agree that it would help the book, and there is a further discussion of this subject. John suggests discussing this with Mr. Matson. Mr. McCormick states that some magazine publication would help the book, especially to have it run in a magazine like *Fortune* and if the book is mentioned, as it would be.]

*Mr. Sloan:* When you get a book and you go to publicize it, do you make any suggestions to the author as to how the book might be improved from the standpoint of merchandising? Or do you leave it to the author?

*Mr. Black:* We are very satisfied with the way the book is now. We usually have to get a book into shape. I can't tell you how much we like it. It's well edited as well as being in good shape. When the Eisenhower book was being written, Mr.

McCormick went to Washington every weekend to straighten out the editing. . . .

*Mr. McCormick:*  Part I of the book is in magnificent form now. There is very little criticism. We could publish it just as it is now.

*Mr. Sloan:*  I am wondering about this. It has come into my mind, as I'm revising the overseas chapter. We have some complex problems and I have thoroughly documented my revisions. John hasn't seen it yet and of course he may not agree. My question is: Are we going into too much detail? Too much documentation?

*Mr. Black:*  Not in this volume [part I]. It is not overdocumented.

[Mr. McCormick and Mr. Sargent say that the documents enhance the book, that they're just right. John points out that part II doesn't have as many documents as part I. Mr. Sloan and Mr. Black touch on questions of illustrations, binding a special edition (Mr. Sloan opposed), the size of the book, and the size of the print.]

*Mr. Black:*  Part I is well proportioned. . . . [He says that if part II were like part I there would be no problems.] We are looking forward to keeping in close touch with your office and we don't anticipate any problems.

[Mr. Sloan raises the question of contact with the publisher. It is agreed that editorial contact would be carried on by Mr. McDonald and Miss Stevens, working with Mr. McCormick, editor-in-chief of Doubleday, and other Doubleday editors. Mr. Sloan would be available at any time.]

This January 15, 1959 meeting with Doubleday, with its enthusiasm on all sides, was the high point in the history of the project. Moore, Sloan's lawyer, approved, Henry R. Luce sent

Sloan a nice letter, and detailed decisions were made in order
to proceed immediately to publication. Seven weeks later, Mr.
Sloan canceled publication to avoid "destroying" General Motors, as he said the lawyers put it to him; his conduct as he did
so was in character, ambivalent and mixed in strategies, much
as he had described himself in his testimony in the Du Pont
trial. So it had been in 1921 when he kept the water-cooled
engine going at the division level while orders from the top were
to install the untried copper-cooled engine in GM cars. So too,
close to home here in 1956, when he backed off signing the first
contract with Doubleday—he did this in response to Moore's
having said that he would never get the book past General Motors. Yet he finessed an understanding with me to complete the
book, which we did to our satisfaction and Doubleday's and,
we thought, without objection from General Motors.

Now in March 1959, with the book done and halted, Mr.
Sloan temporized. In a further discussion of the issues with me
he said that Bruce Bromley of Cravath, the law firm representing General Motors, had read the book and had come to him
requesting its cancellation. Bromley's objection, Mr. Sloan said,
was based in principle on the Supreme Court's adverse ruling
in the Du Pont–GM case, namely, that having the power to
monopolize was sufficient cause to hold against Du Pont: You
didn't have to actually monopolize, Bromley said. Likewise, he
continued, the government's case against General Motors, now
before a grand jury, could eventually go to the Supreme Court
on this issue; based, that is, on General Motors' having more
than fifty percent of the car market. The book, Bromley said,
showed how they had gotten it.

I responded, to Mr. Sloan, that General Motors' share of the
car market was a matter of public record. What did the book
have to do with it? Mr. Sloan said he agreed with me and that

he would take it up with Bromley. When he did so, Bromley replied that there were no particulars; the book showed how General Motors' market power was developed. There is nothing wrong with it, Bromley had said, nothing to correct, we just don't want this book. In the face of Bromley's objection, Mr. Sloan backed off. I wrote in my pocket diary for March 10, 1959: "Book [will] never appear as written after Mr. Sloan is gone."

Speaking to me on a personal level, Mr. Sloan said that he knew this was a great disappointment to me after all the years I had put in on it, and that he wanted to make me a gift of $100,000 in a trust fund that would be payable over ten years. He said that this would have to wait until the next year. On another, more formal plane, he said that he had told his counsel, Moore, about the gift and Moore had said it was very generous, that he, Mr. Sloan, owed me nothing and should take back my rights in the book. But Mr. Sloan was not going to do that.

Notes of a meeting I had with Mr. Sloan on March 28 at his apartment on Fifth Avenue touch on what would become a minefield of issues in our future: his gift, Moore's plans, taxes, and our shares in the book. We discussed the possibility of a new arrangement for what Mr. Sloan termed the "disposal" of his, my, and Catharine Stevens's shares in the book, with figures on potential sales in mind. Mr. Sloan brought up the idea of a trust fund in my name and asked whether I would accept Moore's opinion on the trust's status as taxable income to me. Furthermore, Mr. Sloan distorted Moore's opinion that in any case 100 percent of the rights to the book would go to the Sloan Foundation.

I came away from Mr. Sloan's apartment with the sense that Moore's word "generous" was not in praise of Mr. Sloan's offer to me as much as a criticism of Mr. Sloan's first effort to assist me with my problems resulting from his cancellation of the book. As such it was clever, for Mr. Sloan normally would think that what he had proposed was in fairness, appropriate, a sort of symmetry, whereas generosity would appear as peculiar. The word does not appear in his book's chapter on incentive compensation for the approximately 14,000 bonus executives then in General Motors, where the incentive was pay promised for future performance.

On still another plane, at the office Mr. Sloan proposed that we should wind up the remaining details of the manuscript, as well as possible in the absence of publishers' procedures, but as if we were going to the publisher, after which he hoped Catharine Stevens would stay on with him indefinitely.

We finished the manuscript accordingly, adding the promised appendix consisting of copies of eight documents, seven of them from the period 1919 to 1927, mostly from inside General Motors, expressing concepts of organization, finance, and strategies in the automobile market.

On June 3, Mr. Sloan wrapped up the record in a memorandum to me with the subject title: "Final Review of the General Motors Story, Part I." He led off with: "Points will arise as I make the final examination of the book, now largely finished, and I will pass these on to you in notes for your consideration. This memorandum deals with the following. . . ."

He made three numbered points. In the first he proposed to drop our efforts to get agreement on a footnote describing the legalities of the Du Pont case and instead eliminate it. This was OK with me for the time being. I knew Hogan's controversial views and thought that with conversations back and forth I could expect to get him and the others eventually to agree on a formulation of their positions of disagreement—a bit of unfinished business for the future, if the book had a future.

Mr. Sloan's second point had to do with his anxieties about things in the book "that might work against General Motors." He said he had crossed out two or three sentences—I don't now recall what they were or if I allowed them, in accordance with the policy of the project that I take responsibility for the requirements of the book.

His third point was strategic for the future:

After a certain amount of time passes and we can perhaps have a better idea of what is going to happen in the litigation, if I am still around I intend to raise aggressively the question of publishing the book at some later date. This will involve having it thoroughly analyzed from a legal point of view and perhaps certain deletions made which even under such conditions might appear too dangerous.

As a statement of his interest in the survival of the book as well as of General Motors, this message established common ground between us which would be a determining condition of the book's survival.

In a further landmark step Mr. Sloan wrote, signed, and inserted in the manuscript a listing of the sixteen top General Motors executives who had reviewed it, along with Henry C. Alexander, head of the Morgan Bank, and Walter Carpenter, head of Du Pont, and noting that the facts and figures had been checked by the staff of the New York office of General Motors. "These reviews and checks," he wrote, "were taken into account by Mr. McDonald and myself in preparing the final manuscript. This manuscript reflects the benefit of these reviews and checks, and has my approval. Signed, Alfred P. Sloan, Jr., June 10, 1959."

Bound in two-volume sets, *The General Motors Story* went on the shelf. On occasion Mr. Sloan would, his secretary observed, take his copy down and proudly show it to visitors. And, contrary to Moore's advice, Mr. Sloan had Catharine

Stevens, now his general assistant, file and preserve the records of the project. Copies in my workshop served to keep me on track during the weather to come.

I returned to *Fortune* in September in disgrace. I had inspired a business magazine publisher's dream of promoting a series out of the Sloan memoir, failed, and would now experience the contagion of failure.

I had met *Fortune*'s new managing editor, Duncan Norton-Taylor, when I had returned to the office briefly at the end of the previous year. Physically he was a small man among the generally tall executives of Time, Inc. He had a feeling for language, almost none for business, and was inclined to be stubborn instead of listening when he got fixed on a point—but I may do him an injustice now about when I went in to see him about my salary, for I do not know how much control he actually had in that matter. He had come over from *Time*, along with a couple of other editors, in a sort of Norman invasion of *Fortune*, and so had no memory of my ten successful years there. Taylor was, however, sensitive to the fact that I was arriving back empty-handed. Explanations, reasons, the obvious causes and effects, even the presence of Maurice Moore in a crossover were of no help. "It's 1959," I said. "Why have you set my salary back to where it was when I went on leave in 1954?" "Because you didn't bring back the bacon," said Taylor from across his ME's desk. It didn't matter to him that I had got the job done—twenty-four chapters, the equivalent of twenty-four long middle-of-the-book *Fortune* stories—a copy of which was in his office, as I had sent him a copy of the manuscript. It didn't matter that I had nothing to do with the block to its publication as a book and a series in *Fortune*, nor that it was his chairman and chief counsel Moore who, as Mr. Sloan's lawyer and Cravath partner, had participated in getting Mr.

Sloan to cancel. None of this got through to him. He was not moved. Taylor stuck obtusely to no bacon, no raise, and he signed off with the taunt, "Why don't you sue General Motors?"—a gag that would one day give him pain. As *Fortune* was my market for magazine work, a space to publish in, I went back to work in 1959 under the conditions of 1954 and thought about writing another book on my own if I could get my finances in order.

I went in to see Mr. Sloan at the appointed time in January and found him sitting back impassively, unwilling to talk—an interview absolutely unprecedented and difficult to cope with. What can one say to a putative giver about a gift? I wanted him to understand the magnitude of the disaster on my side: the effect on my career and my personal life of the cancellation of the book and the related setback at *Fortune*. His stiff and uncommunicative posture put me on the defensive. Something was up. I went from being unsettled to upset, to enraged, and left his office in anger.

After this breach of courtesy on both sides, he rebuked me in a conciliatory letter but got the causes in reverse, saying I had entered his office in the mood I left in, an error I corrected in my conciliatory reply. His letter was so very Sloan-like that I quote it in full, with my reply:

January 18, 1960

My dear John,

This refers to your call here in my office last Friday afternoon. As you went out you asked me if I was willing to discuss with you whatever you had in mind. I said no.

In view of the fact that I have always been willing to discuss anything and everything in relation to our contracts for the past five years, this perhaps requires an explanation. The reason I was unwilling to discuss whatever problems you had in mind, just what they are I do not know, was because you entered my office in a very belligerent and highly emotional state of mind. Perhaps you did not realize it. I realized that in such an atmosphere we could not discuss our problems on a cooperative basis in the right kind of climate. It seemed to me therefore the best thing to do was not to discuss them at all, as the result could not help but be prejudicial to a constructive result.

From what I have just said you will imply, very properly, that I am perfectly willing to discuss any problems you wish to raise providing it can be done in a logical and constructive atmosphere. To facilitate this I suggest the following program:

1—That you go over carefully with me the record of the relationships with me, and others perhaps, in connection with the work you have done in promoting [*sic*] "The General Motors Story," making such notes on the records as you would like to have clarified, or dealt with in any other way. I shall do the same thing.

2—Make notes of what subjects, that may be outside the record, that you would like to bring up specifically relating them to any instances that will enable us to develop all the atmosphere possible in their consideration. I shall be glad to do the same.

3—Agree with me that we will not bring up for discussion any problems other than what is outlined on this sort of agenda, I might call it. The purpose of this is not to restrict the discussion but to keep it on the beam, and not digress into channels that have nothing to do with the case, which would only add confusion to what we are trying to accomplish, whatever it may be.

Now I appreciate, and I say this most sincerely, your great disappointment at the status of the five years that we have worked together, as it presently stands. I feel exactly the same way you do about it. While you may contend it means more to you than it does to me, at the same time what it means to me is a great deal but in an entirely different category than what it means to you. Be that as it may. Nothing is going to be accomplished, in view of the fact that we have both experienced a great disappointment as judged by fact today, by your heaping resentment on me, or my finding fault with you. If anything of this kind is to take place it should be addressed to the proper source.

Therefore, let me say any time you are ready to discuss the matter along the lines I suggested above, or in any other way, at a time when it can be done dispassionately and logically, without emotion, and on a factual basis, I will be glad to give you all the time necessary to that end.

Sincerely yours,
Alfred P. Sloan, Jr.

I replied:

January 23, 1960
  Dear Mr. Sloan,
  Thank you for your letter, which arrived while I was away visiting colleges with my daughter.
  I am glad that you are willing to discuss our problems. After working five years together there is every reason for us to have the same good will we have had in the past. I have not thought differently and from my point of view you are mistaken in saying that I entered your office in a "belligerent" state of mind. There is confusion here in cause and effect. I came feeling friendly as always, expecting you to carry out the suggestion you made to me last March. Later I became upset, emotionally if you like, when it seemed that you were repudiating one of the most basic understandings we have had. Perhaps you were not and I am mistaken. Certainly it was an unworthy discussion which I hope we can both forget.
  I know how much the book, being the record of your working life and the story of the great institution, means to you. Like you I trust that sometime it will be published; and whatever I can do to assist you in solving the problems holding it up and in seeing to it that it is properly published when the time comes, I shall of course be glad to cooperate with you in doing.
  As for my problems, they are quite simple. The failure to publish has put a hole in my working life. It is a disaster. Not only have I not benefited as I would have with publication, but now in 1960 I am set back professionally to 1954. Reflect on the effect on your life if in 1926 you had been set back to the circumstances of 1920. You might say I am over twenty-one. And indeed this did not happen to me without forethought. I was forewarned in the summer of 1956 when you rejected the Doubleday contract while it was being prepared. But with your help I took precautions.
  For three months in the Fall and early Winter of 1956 we discussed the issue of cancellation and the consequences for me, twice in an exchange of letters and at other times in person at your office. In December of that year you agreed with me, with perhaps a slightly different emphasis in reasoning, that it would be unwise for me to continue without assurance from you that you would protect me if anything went wrong with publication. You gave me that assurance and counting on it I went on with you to the completion of the project to your satisfaction and mine.

In a discussion with me last March, when you announced to me that we were not then publishing, you recognized the consequences to me and out of a feeling of friendship for me and appreciation you offered me a tax-free gift of $100,000, which you said would happen in January, 1960. I had been counting on that, as I have said, and it was on my mind when I came to your office last Friday.

You suggest in your letter an agenda of three points. Point 1 seems to be a study of the record. From my point of view that is not necessary. It seems that your second point is what is on my mind, as outlined above. Your third point appears to express your desire to narrow the discussion to relevant matters, and I am of course thoroughly in accord.

This being a weekend I am typing this letter myself and on an overworked machine, hence the appearance of the typescript which leaves something to be desired.

It seems hardly necessary to add that it is my wish to be cooperative and constructive as always.

Sincerely yours,
John McDonald

During the next several weeks, we exchanged letters and had talks revolving around my acknowledgment that he had an uncontested right in writing to cancel the book, and my reminding him that he had made an oral commitment, clearly understood by both of us, to protect me from the consequences of such an event—the means, gift, compensation, a negotiated buyout, or whatever, being his choice. In a letter dated March 8, he took the position that my memories referred to conversations which "can only be effectuated when reduced in form and substance and properly accepted by both contracting parties."

At a meeting in his office on March 11, 1960, Mr. Sloan offered me a revised gift of $60,000, payable over ten years (later seven), down from $100,000, he said, because the stock market was down. And, he said, "Mr. Moore says I have an inflated idea of a *Fortune* writer's salary," a revelation memorable in its own right and stunning in context. For the salary in question was my 1954 salary, set back now six years by Norton-Taylor, confidential information tightly held at *Fortune,* purloined by Moore—I trust purloined; otherwise it would have had to be obtained in collusion with a high-level officer of Time Inc.—and put to use here without regard to the passage of time or the accomplishment of the book. The information was also true. As a writer at *Fortune,* I was treated like a monk—much respect, not much money—and labeled so by my friend Elliot Cohen, founder of *Commentary.* The money at that time went to the ranking editors and executives—yet even the managing editor in the forties and early fifties, Ralph Delahaye Paine, upon being moved from editor to publisher said at his farewell editorial staff party, "I feel defrocked." Mr. Sloan may have been misled into believing I made a big salary at *Fortune* by my appearance on the board of editors, a masthead distinction awarded sparingly in those days for performance. The only function of the board of editors was to elect a new member and when that vote was taken the managing editor could say, like Lincoln to his cabinet, you all vote yea, I vote nay, the nays have it. However, at occasional evening dinners it did provide a sort of round table for talking freely about anything, and no managing editor was likely to fire a member of the board of editors for whatever reason without first consulting the editor-in-chief of Time Inc. So there was a tangible value to the distinction. When I was "elected" in 1949, I got no raise in salary; the masthead elevation was the raise. Mr. Sloan may also have been influenced by his opinion of an article I wrote for *Fortune,* published in the December 1953 issue, entitled "How to Get a Raise," in the preparation of which I had consulted him. After it appeared, he wrote me:

When you were in here talking to me the other day, I told you that I had read with great interest your article in the December issue of

*Fortune*—the one that we discussed together at such length—and I was very much impressed with same.

Before I talked with you and within the last couple of days I have had contacts which reflected to me a very favorable reaction on the article. It certainly was a good job done in a very difficult field of analysis because the facts and circumstances are so intangible, so to speak.

Anyway, thanks for giving me the chance to go over it with you and thanks also for a contribution to a better understanding of a highly significant problem.

But the subject of my salary was irrelevant in our negotiations for creating a book and so had never before come up. Moore, on his authority as a top ranking officer of Time Inc., had brought over the salary information as a side service to his client for use in measuring the commensurateness of gift and salary, clinching his advice that the gift was too large for a *Fortune* writer. When Mr. Sloan told me this, I recall just looking at him and imagining a cartoon of the two of them, Daumier figures with heads together, peers in title as chairmen, respectively, of the largest U.S. publisher and largest U.S. industrial corporation, the former slipping the latter the amazing information on a writer's salary. Mr. Sloan, visibly uncomfortable with his source, shrugged, from which I gathered that he acknowledged the impropriety—the damage to his honor as recipient buffered by his telling me about it, which he had not had to do—and as if to say, however, what could he do now but recognize the information as a fact of life and take it into account.

He seemed, however, not to recognize the inversion of the measures he was trying to take. Instead of seeing my return to the *Fortune* salary of 1954 as a negative consequence to me of the cancellation of the book, on Moore's information and advice, he made the setback at *Fortune* a measure warranting further setback. He needed Moore to explain that toboggan effect and Moore didn't; I tried and couldn't. Even so, commensurateness with the achievement of the book, which would have been more to the point, was blocked by the failure to publish; and I could not do anything about it as the hypothetical gift gyrated from $100,000 in March 1959, to zero in January 1960, to $60,000 in March 1960.

But Moore was not yet finished. Having succeeded in imposing an unethically acquired and falsely applied salary measure but having failed to get Mr. Sloan to bargain back my share of the book, Moore made a last-ditch attempt to disqualify the gift. A draft of trust papers of the gift, prepared by him, omitted Mr. Sloan's preparatory oral statements to me that it was a gift in friendship. This was contrary to Mr. Sloan's rule in his letter of March 8 of how our conversations should be "effectuated" in writing.

I pointed out the omission and Mr. Sloan, saying something about taxes—something like for tax reasons?—entered the missing line into the text of the trust, thereby assuring me that it was a gift. I retained my half interest in the book and its subsidiary rights. My half share of the magazine rights had been returned to me in our January 1957 agreement. But it was a long way down from the meeting with Doubleday a year earlier to this degrading scene, and Mr. Sloan wanted no responsibly for the descent.

When I had first complained to Mr. Sloan about his role in the cancellation of the book and he had responded enigmatically that I should complain to the right parties, the advice had seemed no more than a rhetorical device with which he waved me away from him as the responsible person. Then, after our quarrel in his office in January, he wrote me calling it explicitly to my attention that I should look elsewhere for the parties responsible for blocking the publication of the book: "Nothing is going to be accomplished," he wrote, "in view of the fact that we have both experienced a great disappointment as judged by the facts today, by your heaping resentment of me, or my finding fault with you. If anything of this kind is to take place it should be addressed to the proper source."

These words, if rhetorical, had the ring of a logical commandment, rooted in a common disappointment for which he refused to be blamed, and an overlapping interest in what was to become of the book. But to whom was I to complain? In what way? Mr. Sloan's words, however he intended them, remained inoperative until one day an event occurred that made it seem he had something even if he didn't quite mean it that way. I noted it in my pocket diary on February 26, 1960, as "new concept of case." I had lunch that day at the old Biltmore Men's Bar with Frank Donovan, a lifetime close friend and a lawyer from Detroit. He was known among his friends and clients as a brilliant legal analyst with a nonaggressive temperament. No litigator. When we were both twenty, I remember him saying: "When there's a fight, I pick up my hat and go home." He had a large head, somewhat out of proportion to his medium build, and the kind of languid grace that was great for sitting around talking, as we had since our teens. Altogether these characteristics did not quite account for his having been captain of Notre Dame's tennis team under Knute Rockne's athletic directorship and three times tennis champion of Detroit. Less surprising was his making the *Law Review* at Harvard—a sign of the good student he was. He was familiar with legal contests among the automobile companies; among his good friends were a Dodge, a Ford, and others of the motor royalty. He admired Mr. Sloan from a distance, and in general thought well of General Motors, though he had no hesitation as a lawyer in opposing them. He qualified, and if as it is said, character makes plot, as it seems to have with Mr. Sloan in this narrative, aspects of Frank Donovan's character would also have a certain impact on its development. At lunch that day, Donovan said thoughtfully, "Mr. Sloan did not cancel publication of the book. General Motors suppressed it." This remarkable observation was not primarily empirical. It was a legal concept. "Courts," he said, "are becoming interested in damage claims arising from third-party intervention. General Motors intervened to suppress the book for its own interests. A court might well entertain the case of your interest."

If true, this legal concept could make me an active player. In game theory terms I would be able to make moves that would influence the strategic decisions of other players as their moves influenced mine. Coincidentally this would restore my dignity, which had suffered in the recent role of suppliant.

Intuitively, also, as a sort of simulacrum in law of what Mr. Sloan had been saying, Frank Donovan's theory appealed to me. But it was only a theory, and an undeveloped one, and when I took it, as I did right away, to my New York lawyers Fitelson and Mayers, they couldn't see it. So I let it pass at the time.

# II

## Suppression

## 1960–1962

On February 27, 1962, I started suit against General Motors for suppressing Mr. Sloan's book. That day my newly engaged attorney and trial lawyer Edward J. ("Eddie") Ennis telephoned the General Motors legal office and asked where they would like to have my complaint delivered. To Bruce Bromley at Cravath, Swaine, and Moore, they responded. Mr. Sloan, long silent, receded further as lawyers and executives in initial chaos swarmed around the case.

Several things had come together to bring this about. Nearly three years had passed since Mr. Sloan had announced to me the cancellation of publication, and three years was the outside limit for a damage suit. I still did not know what General Motors' problem with the Antitrust Division of the Justice Department had to do with the book. That was still secret and the book was still suppressed with no prospect of publication.

There was a passing episode in early 1961 which I should mention here for its future import. It happened by chance that I was acquainted with Hugh Cox, who was chief trial counsel for the Du Ponts during the many years of the government suit against Du Pont/General Motors. At Christmastime each year from the mid-1950s onward, Hugh, his wife Ethylene Cox, a writer on antique American furniture, and my wife, the painter Dorothy Eisner, and I were house guests of Robert Penn and Eleanor Clark Warren in Fairfield, Connecticut. There would be a dinner party for thirty or forty and an evening of music and dance. We would stay overnight and spend a day or two with the Warrens and Coxes. While the Du Pont trial was on, Hugh did not talk about it; nor did I talk about the Sloan book. But when the Du Pont trial was over, and the Sloan book suppressed, I sent him a copy of the manuscript and after receiving it he asked me to have dinner with him in Washington. He was pleased with the book as American history, and could not see what Cravath had against it, except possibly one line in the Product Policy of 1921: "A monopoly is not planned." On February 23, 1961, he wrote to me as follows: "Today I am sending back to you the book. As I said to you when we dined together I read it with great pleasure and profit. It is a truly fine job and I hope that someday it can be published." Hugh was a distinguished Washington lawyer, a member of the Acheson firm, and a near-miss for the Supreme Court in Truman's administration. He had much experience as an antitrust lawyer in the Justice Department and in private practice, as noted, in charge of the defense of Du Pont, which gave him an intimate familiarity with the affairs of General Motors. The book could hardly have a more perceptive and experienced reader. I would like to have had him for my lawyer, but of course in the circumstances that could not be. His puzzled opinion, however, added to the mystery of why the book was suppressed, and although at that moment it contributed nothing to my understanding of the suppression, it would return.

As it was, having got into this jam, my question was how to get out of it tolerably. I was determined to become a strategic player in the game, as I saw it, with just enough detachment to be rational about it with the only means I had, which was Frank Donovan's concept that General Motors was suppressing and was liable for it. In the absence of my traditional law firm of Fitelson and Mayers, I needed to find another lawyer who would take on the case with skill, willingness, and an interest in developing the legal concept. A good friend of mine, and of Frank Donovan's, offered to engage his own counsel, a famous New York lawyer from a prominent New York law firm, for my case. The friend advised that if this lawyer, a former judge, would agree to take the case I would have the case as good as won. I had to thank him to no end, and also to decline. The concept did not quite fit my strategic sense. For what if the famous lawyer turned it down? I said. My case would be prejudged and I would have to carry that baggage. I preferred to look for someone to try Donovan's legal theory in court or, preferably, to negotiate from the start of such a suit. In any case, this discussion—at lunch in the King Cole room of the St. Regis—played out an aspect of the imagined game and my tenuous position in it.

As Frank Donovan had originally had the legal insight, and was one to think that when he had formulated a concept the other side would see its merits if you gave them time, I wrote him on August 4, 1961, to ask him what he thought of my writing a letter to General Motors; but in the complexities that followed I abandoned this idea. Discussions, however, led to a stronger line of action. As Frank Donovan put it, "GM seems to have abandoned publication altogether. GM's decision. So, we have to talk to Bromley." I read: Sue General Motors. I knew that Donovan thought if Bromley saw his intervention concept, he would fold. My friends at Fitelson and Mayers now looked more closely at Donovan's thinking and began to come around to an appreciation of it in a general way. To study it further with a view to drafting a formal legal complaint, they called in Edward J. Ennis—whom I have mentioned—and Clifford Forster, two distinguished New York lawyers.

Back in the 1930s, after sound had come to film, H. William (Bill) Fitelson and Bertram (Bert) Mayers formed the literary law firm of Fitelson and Mayers (later, with additional partners, the firm came to be called Fitelson, Lasky, and Asian). They mainly represented individuals against institutions: writers, directors, movie and theater stars such as Elia Kazan, Gypsy Rose

Lee, and Mary Martin. Bill, who died in May 1994, was a legend on Broadway, where he was intimately active in the productions of the Theater Guild and represented angels and actors on and off Broadway. They often did run-throughs of plays in the living room of his house on Morton Street, where we and our families lived. He was physically small, excitable, given to staccato speech, sweet and loyal to friends on a personal basis though intimidating at times, pugnacious toward adversaries, and dearly loved by his clients and friends. Our families had been friends for many years, and his firm had reviewed my contracts with Mr. Sloan. So when he saw no light in Frank Donovan's concept of a case against General Motors, and the time was closing in, I had to tell him I was sorry but that it was my intention to find a lawyer of strength and conviction to pursue it. That search became unnecessary after he and his firm changed their minds about Donovan's concept and called in Ennis and Forster.

Eddie Ennis was general counsel of the American Civil Liberties Union (ACLU), later to be its president and chairman. He was lean and breezy and straightforward in speech. He looked like a man who should wear a cap. Eddie was a New Deal Democrat from the 1930s and had spent half of his professional life in public service, the rest at the ACLU; he had been an assistant attorney general at the Justice Department and counsel to the Immigration and Naturalization Service. Clifford Forster, a strong conservative, was doing *pro bono* work at the ACLU, as was Bill Fitelson.

With Frank Donovan in Detroit, Fitelson and Mayers in Hollywood and on Broadway, and Ennis and Forster from public service, my counsel were collectively of pretty wide experience. They were a good team, a match for any in the profession, and perhaps most important for me, they had a feeling for the case.

My friend Dan Seligman, a longtime *Fortune* editor, reminds me that as we now know, my lawyers were not pushing a weak case in law: A theory very like Frank Donovan's, he said, "later became central to one of the biggest business stories of the eighties—the Texaco-Pennzoil-Getty litigation, in which the theory was triumphantly upheld. The parallelism is perfect: You and Sloan had a mutually beneficial deal, as did Pennzoil and Getty. Then Texaco comes along (as GM did), and induces Getty (Sloan) to push aside Pennzoil (McDonald). The courts held against Texaco, of course, and it went bankrupt." As it was, back in the 1960s Frank Donovan was what one of his lifetime law partners would describe as "practically the only genius I ever knew." Donovan continued, "He found solutions to the legal problems other lawyers turned down and said couldn't be done." In the uncertainties of my case, my lawyers were in agreement on the objectives—to require General Motors to release the book or pay damages, and to protect the survival of the book—but the legal issues were complex. A damage suit in a state court would be limited to damages; they debated filing a parallel suit in a federal court for an injunction, which would force General Motors to cease suppressing the book, in which we claimed there was a public interest. However, legal difficulties and Bert Mayers's conviction that federal courts tend to favor institutions over individuals—persuasive to them, although my friend Hugh Cox later commented that Mayers had in fact been mistaken—resulted in limiting the suit to one asking for damages, and in a state court. To bring in the wider objectives, we proposed to sue and to offer to negotiate both the damage and the survival of the book. This was within the private and public concerns of all of us. The survival of the book was also where Mr. Sloan's and my own interests coincided. Most complex legally was General Motors' liability—

new territory in tort law, they agreed. If we did not settle, a court would decide whether the case would be heard and a jury would decide the outcome.

When all decided in early 1962 to go ahead with it, Eddie, Clifford, and I met in Eddie's old-fashioned office at 165 Broadway where they were practicing law together, and we sat around a table for a number of days drafting the complaint together. Employing the same discipline that I would in writing for publication, I did a brief factual history of the project and book. Clifford did the legal research, while Eddie wrote the legal text and prepared himself for his appearance as the presenter of the complaint, the spokesman, the negotiator, and the trial lawyer. We all met in Fitelson and Mayers's office, which was the home base of the suit, to discuss policy and review drafts to the final version of the complaint.

Eddie observed to me sometime early on that I had rights damage, and that General Motors could quickly settle any action that might be brought against them. But there is an embarrassment in this kind of suit—General Motors would still in that case be successfully silencing Mr. Sloan—and thus they could be expected to try to satisfy the damages in some other way. A "vector of faces," he said, in the most elegant description of the relation of the players in and to come into this game.

I worried some about surprising the editors of *Fortune*, though the legal action was a private one unrelated to my work as a writer at the magazine. Mr. Sloan would know through Moore that Time Inc. had nothing to do with my lawsuit; doubtless he had long since surmised it on his own. The complications of telling *Fortune* in advance were formidable. Word would travel from the editorial side to the business side, inevitably to Moore and thence to Cravath, General Motors, and Mr. Sloan, resulting in a free-for-all ahead of time, from my standpoint to no good purpose. Even supposing they could somehow keep it to themselves at *Fortune:* Would the foreknowledge of my suit not be a compromising responsibility? I thought that on balance it was better for them not to know ahead, and instead be surprised and perhaps even dismayed when they learned of it after the fact. Lawsuits were not as common at that time as they have become since; mine could and did shock Time, Inc. But I was ambivalent about notifying my friends and colleagues at Time, Inc., and making them feel they should list one way or the other—evident in notes I made on a lunch meeting in February with Bill Furth, long-time executive editor of *Fortune*. I had written:

Discussed moonlighting. Told him I was looking for some way as my salary is not up to my needs. This led to discussions of the GM book. He asked how long it had been unpublished now. I said it would be three years on March 4th since I knew about it. He said wouldn't that be good occasion to write Sloan about it inquiring whether it could be published. I said March 4th was a dangerous date, that whatever rights I had expired on that date and I had been consulting law firms about my rights with a view to possible action. I said I did not want to put him on the spot by telling him about it and on the other hand I did want to tell. He threw up his hands and said "Don't tell me."

Ennis sent the complaint, as General Motors' legal office had directed, to Bromley at Cravath. The following day, February 28, they discussed it on the telephone. As I remember, Ennis told me that Bromley said, "John is right. We are suppressing. We do not contest the facts in his complaint, but we have good business reasons and the law is on our side."

This was not so surprising, considering that their alternative was to blame the suppression on Mr. Sloan. But it was for us a spectacular beginning of the lawsuit—the core of our case conceded: that GM, not Mr. Sloan, was suppressing, as Frank Donovan and Mr. Sloan himself had seen when it happened.

I remember this event because Bromley was so candid, economical, and also novel in his use of Mr. Sloan's first-name form of address for me, which suggested that the contest would include Mr. Sloan's presence in that relationship. Bromley's subsequent words parallel these: There was no denial that they stopped the book out of antitrust fears. Bromley was also far from sympathetic. He was scornful of the book. "It isn't worth anything," he said. "It's hard reading, and only three people would buy it." He said that it was "monstrous" of me "to do this to an old man." This came to me from a meeting of the lawyers. Cravath was being Cravath, here cool in professional outrage at the return of the book they had buried three years earlier.

## March–July 1962

My lawyers and the GM lawyers met at Cravath the next day, Thursday, March 1, and I went along. Bromley greeted Ennis: "What crook are you defending now?" Legal humor between a judge and the chief lawyer of the ACLU. Bromley and his assistant John Barnum represented General Motors, and Ennis and Mayers represented me. Bromley described their case as a "factual position." The gift, he said, was a payoff, a *"factual* payoff,*"* which was to buy out my interest in the book. He said that Mr. Sloan had had that understanding with me—news to me—and that their taking no release (of my share) was a favor to me as it was in "a tax-free form." Ennis replied that I would not have discussed a buyout for $60,000. So, Ennis reported, they were claiming a misunderstanding with me. Bromley asked whether I knew they were a big advertiser at *Time* and *Life*. They wanted to think about the case some more.

It was, however, as Ennis said, a friendly meeting of the lawyers. They appreciated Ennis's informing them that twenty copies of the book were around. Ennis asked Bromley, "With the highest authorities in General Motors approving the book, how worthwhile is it to stop it?"

Bromley went uptown to see George Brooks, who was the Secretary of General Motors, and the next day Bromley or his assistant, John Barnum, telephoned Ennis on behalf of General Motors to ask for a delay in our proceeding with the suit. Technically, they asked that the summons, but not the complaint, be sent to George Brooks for General Motors. We agreed to grant the delay, the legal arrangement being that we would take back the summons if we were satisfied. Otherwise the summons would constitute service within the statute of limitations and after twenty days the complaint would follow. This legal courtesy arrangement was important, as it provided a space of time in which Time Inc. would intervene and would allow the delay to widen into summer, as we shall see.

Mr. Sloan wanted to have a talk with me. On February 27, the day I began the action, he left a message at my office asking me to call him. The message was followed the next morning by a letter to my home in New York, as follows:

My dear John:

At your convenience, I would like you to come in and see me.

I telephoned your office yesterday and left word to have you telephone me, but, not having heard from you, I thought it advisable to drop you this note.

I first replied that I would call him for an appointment, but on second thought—after discussion with my lawyers—it seemed that no useful purpose would be served by my seeing him at that moment. I wrote him on March 5, 1962:

Since I wrote you that I would call for an appointment, I have talked to my lawyers and they think that we should not have any discussions for the time being. I refrained from advising you of my intentions because I did not and do not wish to involve you in any way.
With warm feelings for you personally.

A week into the pause that we granted General Motors' counsel for them to consider my complaint, Time Inc. entered the game. From notes and memory, their opening gambit went as follows. On March 8, a Thursday, Norton-Taylor called me into his office and said right off: "I want you to withdraw your suit against General Motors."

"Why?" I asked.

"Because you have no legal basis and Sloan gave you a gift of $60,000 in settlement. I think that was a fair settlement."

"How can you say that? What do you know about it to be able to say that?"

Norton-Taylor replied, "I have talked to Del [Ralph Delahaye Paine, former managing editor, now publisher of *Fortune*] and Jack [Jack Dowd, Time Inc.'s inside counsel under Chief Counsel Maurice Moore], and Jack has read the complaint."

"I have five lawyers from three law firms," I responded. "One of them is Frank Donovan from Detroit, who is close to the auto industry. They say I have a good legal case and can win it. Your lawyers are General Motors lawyers. Of course they would say I have no case."

I told Norton-Taylor that I did not know how far we should go in conversation. There was a lawyers' agreement between my counsel and Cravath for General Motors that the case would not be discussed while they were considering it. I told Norton-Taylor that I had wanted to tell him about it the previous week, but was forbidden by my lawyers because of their agreement with Cravath. Now Cravath—lawyers for both General Motors and Time Inc.—had brought it up here. So we talked, and it was a long interview. He wanted me to turn the case over to my "peers"; who they were he didn't say. But I said no and gave him a resumé of the case, my history in it, the gift, and the things Bromley had reportedly said to my lawyers. I pointed out the relation between Cravath and General Motors, Cravath and Time Inc., and Moore and Sloan. I described the incestuous position of Time Inc., which had brought him to put pressure on me. He replied that I should explain this to Del, Jack, and Hedley—Hedley Donovan, who was now editorial director of Time Inc. and heir apparent to Henry R. Luce as editor-in-chief. We discussed that, and also what would happen if we disagreed and they forced me to resign. I said if you hurt me, you will force me to hurt you, and reminded him that Time Inc. *should* be neutral.

Norton-Taylor asked if I would be satisfied if General Motors allowed the book to be published. I said yes, that publication of the book would wash out the large part of my complaint, the rest being to restore the status quo with the publisher and such matters. Norton-Taylor said that the whole case was more complicated than he had thought, and that he would talk to Del. He advised me to do the same.

Del Paine and I had been friends ever since he had hired me when he was managing editor in 1945. I called him the following Monday morning, March 12. He said that we had better meet that day, and that I should call him after lunch to set the time. When I did so he said we had better meet soon: "I am trying to get them [the powers at Time Inc.] to keep their shirts on, but I don't know how long I can do it." A half-hour later we met in his office.

I apologized. "I didn't tell you beforehand because I thought the knowledge would implicate you—although I almost told

Bill Furth." Del said, "You know what we're worried about—advertising." I said: "Your not knowing of my suit should protect you. After the lawyers met, it was contrary to their agreement for me to talk about it." Del said: "Tex Moore. This affair is riddled with conflict of interest."

Del wanted to know my story. I told him roughly: Mr. Sloan's position to defer the book, General Motors' decision to kill it. Bromley's buyout view of the gift, news to me; Mr. Sloan's telling me that he did not want to buy me out. The gift history: Mr. Sloan's proposal, the $100,000–$60,000 offer—no bargaining. My keeping my half-ownership; the history of GM's cooperation in the book, contributing to and checking the facts; Mr. Sloan's approval; the agreement with Doubleday to publish; General Motors' intervention as we were on our way to the publisher with the manuscript.

Del asked whether I had a legal case against Mr. Sloan's right to cancel. "My case is against General Motors," I said, "not Mr. Sloan. My lawyers—from three different law firms—say I have a case. I can't discuss the legalities. Objectively my case is on Mr. Sloan's side. They will have to explain to him that the book is dead; I am for publication."

Del asked if publication would satisfy me. I said yes, assuming that we could get back the conditions of three years ago. "I want publication," I said, "and I had to sue for damages." I explained that the lawyers' arrangement was to serve the summons, not the complaint, at Bromley's request. This legal distinction was an important one: This provided time for discussion between General Motors' lawyers and mine. If we got a satisfactory settlement, we would take back the summons and the suit would be off.

I asked what Time Inc.'s interest was. "Well, you know," Del responded, "advertising." I said that that was what Bromley had asked my lawyer Ennis in what now seemed mock surprise: "Doesn't John know we are big advertisers at Time Inc.?" I told Del that I did not want to get Time Inc. into trouble, and did not expect or require them to come out on my side. I thought they should be neutral. As a case under the law of torts, this was not employer-employee business, and it would be bad procedure for Time Inc. to take sides in the matter or pressure me. "What would Donner [chairman and chief executive of General Motors] think about it?" Del asked. "Rationally," I answered, "Donner should agree. It would be bad for General Motors to pressure Time Inc." Del said that he agreed with me, because there was too much conflict of interest in every direction, and that he would try to obtain that policy for Time Inc. But he added, "I don't know if I can."

Del said the Justice Department could issue a subpoena for the book. "Yes," I answered, "but they haven't." We talked about there being two hundred or more people who had read all or part of the book. "How can they hope to suppress it?" Del asked.

"The book is not about Mr. Sloan's private life," I said, "it's about his public life, which was almost all his life." I said the book contained about 225,000 words—not garbage, a *Fortune* "corporation story" on a large scale—and its factual details had been checked for accuracy by us as well as by GM. Del said that *Fortune* had an interest in publishing a several-part series from the story. We talked for an hour or an hour and a half, and in the end left the matter open for further talk.

A couple of days later Del called in another *Fortune* writer and close friend we had in common, Herbert Solow, to discuss the case further as a sort of go-between. Herbert reported back to me on the substance of their talk. Del, it seemed, had changed his position overnight. Time Inc. was not worried about GM advertising but felt that it had a public relations interest in my case. For one thing, if it was litigated, there would be publicity that a *Fortune* editor was suing GM. Thus they wanted to understand the situation in order to try and find a solution that would be satisfactory to both GM and me. Del thought I should get a settlement with GM and get it spread over time, and that there was nothing strange about the idea of a gift. Publication had been deferred with damage to the editor, so the author, Mr. Sloan, after rejecting buyout, decided to make a gift in lieu of publication. Unilateral. No bargaining. Del had wondered about arbitration, but thought the book trade "too flabby" to make arbitration worthwhile.

Del seemed to be the one appointed to handle the situation for Time Inc. and he wanted to find a solution, to put the fire out, to find a way to get the summons withdrawn without a loss of position on the statute of limitations. Del thought that Time Inc. should disentangle themselves from the Cravath conflict of interest, removing Tex Moore from the scene, and that they should engage an independent counsel who could talk to my lawyers and find out what my legal case was. Del said, "We will talk to Donner. He's a sensible man. Conditions have changed over the last four years. The Du Pont case is settled. Take another look at this. Our new lawyer will meet with the lawyers for both sides."

Thursday evening, March 15, Norton-Taylor called me at home and said, "We—that is—Time Inc. is calling in outside counsel for this whole matter. We want to free ourselves from the Cravath point of view and get some independent advice. I don't know who it is, but I expect you will be hearing from him. You said neutrality. Pretty hard to do. Our involvement is pretty deep. [We g]ot outside help."

The next day, Friday the 16th, Del sent for Herbert and informed him that their lawyer would be John Garrison of Lord, Day, and Lord. The lawyer was chosen by Hedley Donovan. Herbert passed this information on to me.

When I heard from Hedley Donovan—in his new capacity as Time Inc.'s editorial director—on Monday the 18th, I knew that meant Del had been withdrawn from the case. Donovan said that he would like to get together with Jim Linen, president of Time Inc., and me the next morning at ten o'clock regarding the litigation with GM. "As you know," he said, "we have retained Lord, Day, and Lord in order to obtain a dispassionate point of view. We talked to them yesterday, Jim Linen too: several conversations." I said, "Your lawyers should talk to mine. They will listen. I have no problem with Time Inc." We met the next morning at ten.

The meeting was grim and hurried, and lasted perhaps ten or fifteen minutes. Hedley sat behind his desk, his eyes milky as they sometimes got when he rolled them into a stern, steely focus. Linen stood nervously to the side on my right, the three of us points in a Pinteresque triangle of tension. We were not strangers: Hedley and I had come to *Fortune* at the same time, in 1945, he to go the editor route, slated now to succeed Luce as editor-in-chief. Until this moment we had been good personal and professional friends, despite some strains over his editorial policy at *Fortune*. Linen began, saying what I knew: They had engaged lawyers in the firm of Lord, Day, and Lord to represent them in my case in order to avoid their obvious conflict of interest in having the same lawyers as General Motors.

"Who are they?" I asked.

Hedley answered: "John Garrison and Herbert Brownell."

"Brownell?" I said. "Dewey's man?" (A local New York identification, as Dewey and Brownell were political associates in the East Coast liberal wing of the Republican Party.) Linen drew himself up and said, giving Brownell his full, formal title: "The former attorney general."

It was an impressive announcement. Brownell, as Eisenhower's chief domestic political strategist, had guided Eisenhower's victory over Senator Robert Taft for the Republican nomination in 1952. After his election Eisenhower appointed him attorney general—Brownell's own choice among several cabinet positions; as he had explained to the president, "I am a lawyer." It was also clever of Time Inc. to engage him as a special counsel in my case, for Brownell in public office had been the outstanding antitruster in the country. He had started the antitrust investigation of General Motors that had reached the stage of grand jury proceedings in 1959. Some good and well-placed players were coming into my game.

Hedley said that Garrison and Brownell had formed an opinion about my case, its negative effect on my professional standing, and how much I could keep under the tax laws if I won. After delivering these statements, he said that they had advised Time Inc. to do nothing at that time. There was some discussion about my effort to inform Bill Furth, who was now on a "hot seat." Donovan wished I had told him. "Time Inc. is in it," he said, "because of your leave of absence, the magazine rights, and the fact that you are a *Fortune* editor." He and Linen repeated emphatically: "We're in it." They asked me if I would see their lawyers. I said I would, on the condition that my lawyers were present.

I asked if Lord, Day, and Lord had seen the complaint. Hedley said of course, and that they had talked to Cravath. I said, "How could they draw conclusions without talking to my lawyers and hearing my side?" I added that Cravath had told my lawyers that the gift was a "factual buyout," and Bromley had asked, didn't I know they are big advertisers at Time Inc.? So what could Lord, Day, and Lord understand without my side?

Hedley said, "That's what we are doing, but not exactly."

He said Time Inc. paid a lot of legal fees to Lord, Day, and Lord and I might as well take advantage of it.

Snarled implications ensued. Paine, speculating that General Motors might mistakenly think that Time Inc. was involved and, in reprisal, withdraw advertising, had thought this could be averted by talking to Donner, who was "a sensible man." Now Paine and *Fortune* had been removed from the scene. Donovan and Linen, acting officially for Time Inc. at the corporate level, were saying that they were implicated by my having done the book, hence they were responsible for my conduct in suing General Motors. In their view I was implicated as a writer by appearing to "be" *Fortune,* upgraded, as it were, from mere writer to representative. And so now they had it worked out that it was not GM's advertising in Time Inc. that was at stake; what was at stake was my professional standing—my job. Confronted with this, I might think twice about continuing my suit against General Motors. But I thought differently: I thought about suing Time Inc. And I thought that it would make some sense, however unpalatable, to recognize that Tex Moore reveled in conflict of interest as a way of life, representing all at once: Time Inc., Mr. Sloan, Cravath, and General Motors, any of whom in their mode of operation could expect that Moore would be able somehow to continue to deal me out.

With all these connections, Tex Moore was the unseen presence at the meeting. Though excluded from physical appearance by his Cravath connection, he was still chief counsel of Time Inc. and a member of its board of directors. As Mr. Sloan's lawyer he was the primary source and fabricator, as well as operator and teller, of the story they were getting back in a simulation from Lord, Day, and Lord. Furthermore, he was a member of the family of a family company; Tex had a lock on this matter at Time Inc.

Donovan and Linen made it clear that they had not called me in to discuss the merits of my case but to inform me of their special counsel's threatening opinion of it and to obtain from me an agreement to meet Brownell and his associate John Garrison at Lord, Day, and Lord. Linen was in a hurry. He said something as they left about taking the results of this meeting to some other meeting.

The only knowledge I had of an overt General Motors threat to Time Inc. was Bromley's remark to Eddie when he first learned of my suit: "Doesn't John know we are big advertisers at Time Inc.?" There was precedent for the anxiety, for General Motors, a few years earlier, had withdrawn advertising from the *Wall Street Journal* in reprisal for the *Journal* having jumped the gun on the then-customary release date for information on General Motors' new car models. I met Harlow Curtice, then president and chief executive of General Motors, at a General Motors affair at the University Club in New York and said to him: "You shouldn't have done that." He replied, "What could I do? They spoiled the sales of current models we were still closing out." I said nonspecifically: "You need a different strategy."

It was not a minor crisis at the top of Time Inc. But was the issue real or imagined? My friend Jack Jessup, chief editorial writer for *Life,* told me matter-of-factly that a large part (he said fifteen percent) of *Life's* revenue came from Pontiac. *Life's* losing the account was not something I wanted to have happen. For *Life/Fortune/*Time Inc. were not responsible for my having done the book, nor were they even remotely responsible for my suit. But they were responsible for Tex Moore, whom they could expect to oblige GM by canceling the book and the new suit. I wanted the book; the rest was not my business. Luce, one would think, had enough advertising "patrons" to make him immune to fears of losing one in an attack. Why should Luce, the leading magazine publisher in the United States, be afraid of General Motors? Why shouldn't General Motors be equally afraid of him? For presidential hopefuls, senators, and governors, an invitation to lunch with Luce at Time Inc. was a command, yet here he was, being represented as in a panic over his presumed rogue editor suing the biggest advertiser in the country.

There was no question but that Time Inc. wanted to fire me in order to appease GM; I later learned from Time Inc.'s house counsel, Jack Dowd, that for some of them, the sooner the better. Much as it pained Hedley, if the time came, he would, it appeared, as crown prince to Luce, have had trouble not going along. But they could not do so prudently in their own self-interest without the kind of combined legal and moral cover that Brownell, with his high authority, provided them. His advice to wait suggested willingness on his part, as their lawyer, to defend them in the future against a suit by me that would have to follow their firing me and that would be less cool, less civil, altogether a bloodier encounter than a plain showdown with General Motors. I thought of the writer Harold Nicholson, sitting next to a window of a train on his way home, looking out across an ominously rising river and being taken with a perverse wish to see it overflow its banks. Likewise I wished the executives of Time Inc. would go ahead and do their worst, thereby giving me the pleasure of letting them have it. Other emotionally satisfying but less operational musings, such as going public, were restrained by the objective of getting the book out. I couldn't get it out without Mr. Sloan.

When I went into the Fitelson and Mayers office with the news that they would be facing Brownell, Bill cried, half mockingly, "Maybe *we* should get an attorney general, too." But, though put on their mettle, they were not fazed.

On May 28 my first confrontation with Brownell took place at Lord, Day, and Lord's office at 23 Broadway. Present were Brownell and Garrison for Time Inc., Ennis and Mayers for me, and myself. Ennis had had a preliminary meeting, where he found them to be unemotional about the matter. Garrison remarked that it was unusual for them to represent an employer (Time Inc.) in a situation where an employee (McDonald) was suing a customer (General Motors)—an observation that implicitly recognized Time Inc.'s stake in General Motors' advertising. Mayers asked Brownell, politely, what his legal place was in the matter before us, and Brownell said something to the effect that it was not clear. He repeated what I had been told at Time Inc.: that he was called in because of the conflict of interest that was represented by Cravath being the attorneys for both Time Inc. and General Motors. Brownell affirmed that he had advised Time Inc. to do nothing about me until it was over. Brownell wanted to talk about the case, taxes, and my professional standing. There was a question, he said, of whether Time Inc.'s relation to me and mine to them would be injured. He had heard the other side, and now he said he wanted to hear mine. Brownell raised a question as to whether the gift was valid. As my notes of the meeting read:

Whether Trust [the gift] would be jeopardized if the case went to court and everything tried. . . . I said if Trust [were] challenged I would fight. . . . I told the story. . . . I said if anyone attacked or injured my professional standing I would answer. My professional standing rests on my writing. I am a writer. [This is] my first experience in the law [a law case]. Don't know what a lawyer would do. As a writer, I would answer and write the entire case in detail with the documents.

Brownell requested the second meeting for the morning of July 9. He would then meet with Time Inc. executives if he had not already done so, to give them the report he had given me and my lawyers. The date was more convenient for him than for me, as he was in New York intending to go abroad, and I was on vacation on Cranberry Island, Maine; but he was calling the tune at the moment, and so I made the trip to New York to meet him. The same cast of characters: Brownell and Garrison for Time Inc., Ennis and Mayers for me. Brownell had reached his conclusions: General Motors had good business reasons for suppressing the book, those being in the areas of public relations, legislation, and antitrust. On the other hand, he said I did not have good reasons for suing General Motors: I had no legal case, and it would give me tax problems surrounding the gift. Furthermore, my professional standing was in jeopardy. He said I was "shaking the tree"—a metaphor for his opinion that I had been adequately rewarded and was suing just to get more money. Mayers asked him what Mr. Sloan's attitude was. Brownell, moving his hand sideways, wavelike, said, "Yea-nay."

With everybody doing my taxes for me—Del Paine ("spread the damage payment"); Hedley Donovan ("How much will you have left if you win?"); and Brownell ("shaking the tree")—I asked Brownell, "Are you trying to say that Mr. Sloan and I conspired to cheat the Internal Revenue Service?" Brownell turned to my lawyers and said: "McDonald will win before a jury."

## July–September 1962

Despite the implications of that concession—for a jury trial was what it would be—Brownell, in his capacity as a special counsel and in the style of a special prosecutor, defended General Motors' suppression of the book, held against my complaint, and condemned me morally for the action.

And so, to review again Brownell's judgment, which would be Time Inc.'s position: General Motors was justified in suppressing the Sloan book, for three good business reasons. One, the book would harm General Motors in its actual or potential antitrust litigation with the government; two, it could bring on legislation harmful to General Motors; three, it would be bad for General motors' public relations. Brownell provided no particulars about how the book would bring these harms to General Motors. And as for me, Brownell held that I had no case in law; that I had been paid off and was "shaking the tree," and that if I persisted in suing General Motors I would injure my professional standing as a writer and an editor of *Fortune;* as I read it, ipso facto, that would be the end of that career.

In 1954 Brownell, as the U.S. Attorney General, had started the major antitrust investigation of General Motors, which was still ongoing; now, in matters of law, legislation, and public relations, he found that General Motors was justified in suppressing Mr. Sloan's book. This revolving-door action looked at first sight like a fine propitiatory gift for Time Inc. to have offered General Motors in order to ward off reprisal for my suit, except for the implication that with the suppression so justified, the book must contain a guilt to be suppressed. Why suppress an innocent book? Still, Brownell's legal good will toward General Motors on behalf of Time Inc., combined with his threat to my job at Time Inc., formed Time Inc.'s shield against the real or imagined threat from General Motors.

Before the meeting ended, Brownell out of the blue announced a major turn of events to which he was privy while we until that moment were not. He said: "General Motors will defend." Two hours later that afternoon, General Motors returned the summons, the official legal sign that they would litigate the case. Heavy collaboration between Lord, Day, and Lord for Time Inc. and Cravath for General Motors was thus brazenly laid on as the action shifted from the Time Inc. flank to the General Motors front.

Under the truce reached by General Motors' lawyers and mine, General Motors was given time to consider how they wanted to respond to the suit. On February 28, Ennis, as noted, had sent General Motors the summons but not the complaint. Their move was either to return the summons and receive the complaint, meaning defend in court, or alternatively to "satisfy the complaint" legally by paying or negotiating the damages. Now, after they had stretched this time period through excuses to several months and following the Time Inc. division, they had, on July 9, returned the summons—which meant, as Brownell had notified us, that General Motors was prepared to fight it out in court.

I returned to Cranberry Island and wrote two letters to my lawyers regarding the strategic situation that had been left by the set of meetings with Brownell. The first, to Bert Mayers, is dated July 14, 1962.

Cranberry Island, Maine
   Friday, July 14, 1962
   Dear Bert,
   I don't know how to evaluate this point but I offer it to you and Bill and Eddie for your consideration. We have so far rested the evidence of General Motors' suppression of the book on the Hogan letter to Sloan in, I believe, June of 1959. Brownell defends the suppression as motivated by good business reasons, namely, public relations, the avoidance of possible legislation leading to the dissolution of General Motors, and antitrust. My impression was that under pressure from

you and Eddie he was a bit shaky about the antitrust aspect. The point I want to offer, for what it is worth, is that the original suppression of the book was not motivated by such generalized reasons, but specifically by a Grand Jury action of the Antitrust Division of the Justice Department in, I believe, the fourth week in January, 1959. Eddie should have in his files some newspaper clippings which give the exact date and nature of the proceeding. Sloan informed me a few weeks later that owing to this government action, General Motors had given the book to Bromley to review. On March 4, Sloan told me that Bromley for General Motors objected to the publication of the book and requested the cancellation of the arrangements then underway with Doubleday for publication. Sloan said that Bromley's request was motivated as follows: The government suit for the severance of Du Pont from General Motors had been decided in the Supreme Court on the issue of power; that is, ownership by Du Pont of twenty-three percent of GM's stock gave Du Pont the power as a supplier to General Motors to control GM's purchasing and was therefore in restraint of trade, whether or not any abuse of that power had occurred (the court also said that the abuse had occurred, but that this was not necessary to the decision). Bromley, according to Sloan, reasoned that the government's new action against General Motors (the one begun in January, 1959) would eventually be decided in the Supreme Court on the same principle: power. In this case the power would be fifty percent of the car market (fifty-six percent in 1962). The book showed how General Motors' power was developed and must be suppressed to keep it from the government.

I said to Sloan that if the courts rule against this power, General Motors is dead. But that power is a matter of public record. What's the book got to do with it? Mr. Sloan said, I agree with you. I don't understand Bromley. I said, ask Bromley for the particulars against the book. He said he would. He did and reported back to me that Bromley said there were no particulars; only that the book showed how General Motors' power was developed.

Soon after this Bradley came to me and said that Tex Moore wanted the research files of the book to be destroyed. Bradley said that Moore apparently had not been able to get this message over to Sloan, and Bradley asked me if I would take that [Moore's proposal] up with Sloan. I said I would but that I would oppose the destruction of the files as this would undermine the validity of the book if future scholars wanted to verify any particular fact in the book. I went to Sloan and

reported to him the Moore-Bradley message, together with my objections. Sloan said he agreed with me and we would leave the files
alone.

Not too long afterward the government went to court to seek a subpoena for GM documents back to 1929. The court rejected the request
as being too vague. Later the government made a more modest request
and I do not know where the action now stands. Sloan hoped it would
blow over and expected in any case that he would work out his objective of limited postponement of publication.

The Hogan letter in June expanded General Motors' objection to
the book to include its relation to all present and future litigation and
legislation. This could hardly mean postponement, or even Brownell's
euphemism "indefinite postponement." It read to me like permanent
suppression. The question, however, was whether Sloan's or Hogan's
view would prevail. The passage of time has shown that Hogan's view
is controlling.

I went along with Sloan's idea of limited postponement while he
tried to work something out. As you know, I am not willing to accept
suppression of the book if there is anything I can do about it.

It is the opinion of high authority that this book is an important
contribution to American history. It describes not only the development of the largest industrial corporation in the United States but the
development also of the basic concepts of big business in product, financial, and organizational policies. Through GM alone it deals with
the production and distribution of two percent of the Gross National
Product. I wonder whether the public would agree with Brownell that
it is good business to keep this history secret, and whether the Congress
of the United States would agree that it is good business to keep this
information from the House and the Senate as they deliberate legislation. As for antitrust, if the book is presumed to reveal illegal activities,
what is the right to suppress it? If it does not reveal illegal activities,
what's the objection? Here these people are controlling vast areas of
the U.S. economy and they argue for the secrecy of their whole past
like outlaws, or [Soviet] Russians.

The point of this note is whether any weight should be given to the
fact that the suppression of the book was first motivated by the desire
of GM to keep its contents from the Antitrust Department in a specific
action which had been started. We have dealt so far only with the
second phase of their motivations as expressed by Hogan to Sloan and
Brownell to us.

In a second letter, to Bill Fitelson on July 16, I wrote:

Dear Bill,

I'd like to clarify a little better the line of thought I spoke to you about this morning. I only advance it as a possible course, as I can not myself see all of its implications.

As background first, Brownell said GM will defend and his report probably clarifies the present GM defense. The report was made in a form very much like a GM brief. GM has Brownell's support and his formulation of the case. Immediately upon his presenting it to us, GM returned the notice of appearance.

Brownell argued that GM only secured the indefinite postponement of the book, and for good business reasons, and Sloan had the "yea, nay." As for my action, he and Garrison stated that I was only "shaking the tree." This was presumably one aspect of the threat against my professional standing. Bert, in his reply to Brownell, said that Brownell was contending that I was making a "strike suit," and that Brownell was mistaken. Bert said that I sought publication and would not accept any settlement that did not include some provision against the permanent suppression of the book.

Now GM has had an opportunity to settle primarily by publication and, it appears, has considered it and declined.

The question on my mind is: How can I avert the impression they will try to give that I am "shaking the tree"? If they think they can make that impression and threaten me with it, they will count this as a strength against me, especially at Time Inc. They might even be encouraged to litigate. And Time Inc. might be encouraged to act against me. Is this not possible?

On the other hand, if we revise the complaint and return to the earlier conception of injunction relief as well as damages—whatever weaknesses the injunction effort might have, which we must consider—would it not at least have the merit of making clear and definitive my aims in the case?

I don't say that this will necessarily reach the stage of litigation in court. Its value, if any, lies first of all in its effect immediately upon service of the complaint. Would it not disarm them with respect to their "shaking the tree" contentions, block this contention in the Brownell report, and perhaps persuade Time Inc.? It is possible that Time Inc. will, in opposing me, defend GM's right, on the grounds of Brownell's "good business reasons," to suppress the book (or "indefinitely" postpone it). But I wonder whether such "good business reasons" will appeal to Luce, himself a publisher, and whether he would like to get into the position where he would have to defend suppression. And if Time Inc. cannot oppose me, perhaps GM cannot. Might this not then force opening the door to negotiations for immediate publication or at least for setting a future date for publication with economic redress for the loss of income?

There is also the surprise effect.

And there is in my mind the thought that one day I may have to defend myself by writing and publishing the story. In that event, would not the injunction effort make my position objectively clear—instead of my having to explain it by logical inference from the damage suit alone?

Perhaps I am mistaken somewhere in this line of thought, and even if I am correct, there may be other counterbalancing effects of an injunction clause that are not desirable. For example, when we discussed this course a few months ago, someone raised the question of whether GM could not pretend to withdraw its objections to publication and privately prevail on Sloan to carry the ball, so that guarantees would have to be obtained. This would be all right in negotiations, but a court cannot publish the book or perhaps even assure its publication.

However, I put this out for reconsideration in view of the way things are now.

On July 24 Eddie Ennis wrote a letter to Brownell, setting forth my case legally, historically, and factually through to recent events:

The more I reflect on our last meeting on this matter on July 9th with Mr. Garrison and Mr. Mayers, to which Mr. McDonald was brought from Maine, the more disappointed I am to realize that the purpose of the meeting was not to ascertain any more facts but merely to summarize your view presumably to be transmitted to Mr. McDonald's employer. Frankly, Mr. Garrison's summary sounded to us entirely similar to the position of General Motors and failed, we believe, to give any recognition to the legal and equitable merits of Mr. McDonald's claim. Consequently it is my belief that fairness to Mr. McDonald requires that the report to his employer also include a full statement of the facts and equities of his position which I take the liberty to summarize as follows:

From 1954 to 1959 Mr. McDonald, on leave of absence as a member of the Board of Editors of *Fortune* and pursuant to written agreement with Alfred P. Sloan, Jr., then Chairman of the Board of Directors of General Motors, worked with Mr. Sloan on the research and writing of the book entitled "The General Motors Story," which is the history of the growth of General Motors. By agreement Mr. McDonald has a 50% interest in the proceeds of the publication of the book (originally subject to an option by Time Inc. on the magazine rights).

There can be no question of the public interest in the publication of a complete history of General Motors' growth and activities. No other complete history of General Motors has been written although it is the largest industrial enterprise in the United States, which produces approximately 2% of the gross product of the United States. Such experienced publishers as Doubleday & Co., on the basis of the first three chapters written, offered an unprecedented royalty of $50,000 against the book rights alone and characterized the book as:

*A document in American social and economic history as significant in its own way as "The Education of Henry Adams" is in American cultural history and as the Federalist Papers in our early economic and political history. The General Motors story is likely therefore to be neither a company history nor a business book in the usual sense but a major item in our national record.*

In 1959, when the book was completed and ready for publication, Mr. Black, president of Doubleday, stated, at a conference to arrange final details of publication, that the book would be looked upon not only as a story of General Motors or an important business book, but an important contemporary history.

The point has been made that Mr. Sloan in his contract with Mr. McDonald retained the right to make the decision as to whether the book should be published. That decision was made in the affirmative by Mr. Sloan, who completed all of the arrangements with Doubleday, including the publication date and even the selection of the binding and the type face and other details of the publication.

Then came the act of the suppression of the book by General Motors. On May 27, 1959, Mr. Hogan, General Counsel for General Motors, wrote Mr. Sloan: ". . . I do, of course, recall my general comment about the book and my concern that there were many parts of the book which could be used against General Motors in connection with its present and probable future antitrust litigation and legislation. . . ." It is undeniable that were it not for the action of General Motors, the book would have been published. It would have been simple for Mr.

Sloan to have provided in his contract with Mr. McDonald that the consent or approval of General Motors was necessary before publication of the book. The contract does not so provide, and conspicuously absent from the contract is any reference to General Motors. The decision was Mr. Sloan's to make and he made it in favor of publication in the most emphatic fashion by his arrangement with Doubleday.

Mr. Sloan's decision to publish the book was then overruled by the pressure of General Motors.

It must be emphasized on behalf of Mr. McDonald that no claim is being made against Mr. Sloan, but only against General Motors for unjustified suppression of the book after the highest officials of General Motors cooperated in the preparation of the book. When the book was completed General Motors approved its factual accuracy.

At that point, when the book was ready to be delivered to Doubleday, General Motors suddenly changed its position and decided to suppress publication of the book for reasons wholly apart from its factual accuracy. It is not disputed that suppression of the book caused Mr. McDonald serious monetary, as well as professional, damage.

The Du Pont anti-trust litigation, commented on by Mr. Hogan in his letter of May 27, 1959, to Mr. Sloan, involving Du Pont's acquisition of General Motors stock has, of course, been concluded but the suppression of the book upon grounds of possible antitrust complications for General Motors continues unabated. It is, to say the least, very difficult to contemplate that any court will hold General Motors legally or morally justified in suppressing a factually accurate account of its beginning and growth written by its chief executive officer because of fear of antitrust complications. Surely the public interest, as well as Mr. McDonald's interest, forbids suppression of the book on any such basis. The applicable decisions of the courts make it clear that the defendant's conduct which so injures the plaintiff is a *prima facie* tort.

There has been some discussion of the fact that following General Motors' suppression of the book, Mr. Sloan made a gift to Mr. McDonald. It has been implied that this gift in some way should be considered as full remuneration to the plaintiff for his rights in the book and that, therefore, he should not seek damages for its suppression. But Mr. Sloan made it clear at the time of the gift that he would not negotiate to purchase the plaintiff's rights in the book and was making a unilateral gift and that the amount and conditions of the gift were entirely for his decision and not for negotiation.

No suggestion was made by Mr. Sloan that this gift involved a purchase of Mr. McDonald's rights. No attempt was made by Mr. Sloan to obtain a release from Mr. McDonald of his rights, or an assignment of his rights, although it may be assumed that the very able lawyers acting for Mr. Sloan (Cravath, Swaine & Moore), as well as Mr. Sloan, certainly were aware of the legal, moral and equitable consequences of such an assignment or such a release. On the contrary, Mr. Sloan emphatically denied any desire for a release or assignment of Mr. McDonald's rights.

The passage of time now compels the conclusion that General Motors neither in March 1959, when it stopped publication of the book, nor up to the present time has sought temporary delay in publication. General Motors' position apparently is that the book is permanently suppressed and it has pursued this position even to the extent that it suggested to Mr. McDonald and Mr. Sloan that the records which they had collected and preserved in the course of the research and upon which the book is based should be destroyed. Mr. Sloan refused to do so because, of course, these records supply the verification for the book and will be invaluable to any research based on the book.

In our conferences it has been suggested as a proper basis for Time's interest in the merits of the claim against General Motors that Mr. McDonald's professional reputation as a writer and as an editor of *Fortune* may in some way be involved in his suit against General Motors. The fact is that he was on leave of absence from *Fortune* when he worked with Mr. Sloan on the preparation of the book so that his position as editor of *Fortune* is in no way involved. Moreover, his reputation as a well-known writer on business is not in any way impaired by his efforts against suppressions of the book. On the contrary, it must be emphasized that as an established writer interested in having his work published Mr. McDonald's professional integrity dictates that he fight against this suppression of the book. It could be questioned only if he cravenly acquiesced in the suppression of five years of his professional work because General Motors, or other parties, attempt to persuade him supinely to surrender.

Finally, it should be appreciated that all of Mr. McDonald's efforts have been directed to procuring publication of the book. His profession is writing for publication and no amount of damages can wholly compensate him for permanent suppression of the product of several years of professional work. His action against General Motors was instituted on counsel's advice only when it became clear to him that

General Motors did not intend the book to be published at any time and that his only remedy was a suit for damage against General Motors upon which the statute of limitations was about to expire, if he did not commence the suit at once. He and his counsel have taken the minimum action necessary to protect his rights. The summons was served on General Motors on March 2, 1962, and no further action has been taken by him pending conferences first with General Motors attorneys and then with Time's special counsel in the hope that General Motors could be persuaded to permit publication of the book which both Mr. Sloan and Mr. McDonald and many other persons believe reflects great credit on General Motors.

We have all recognized your unusual position as special counsel to report to Mr. McDonald's employer on the merits of his action against a third party. I now trust that the facts, the law and equity from a point of view of Mr. McDonald will be adequately covered in the final report of your survey of the matter. It is respectfully submitted that the professional standing and integrity of Mr. McDonald compel the very course of action that he has taken, and compel resistance against pressures of any kind.

Professional courtesy would ordinarily have brought some sort of answer from Brownell. But to my knowledge, Ennis did not receive a reply from Brownell other than an acknowledgment from his office that Ennis's letter had been received in Brownell's absence. Nor did I hear anything more from Time Inc. I continued to write for *Fortune* in internal exile, a cold atmosphere at the brass level with the exception of Assistant Managing Editor Dan Seligman, who made a point of showing his continuing friendship in the halls and outside despite my warning him that I was poison.

On July 26, Ennis served the complaint on General Motors, and the war was on the main front. The lineup would be Bromley, with Barnum and perhaps others at Cravath as trial lawyers for General Motors. Behind them, controlling the legal strategies inside General Motors, would be Al Powers, Henry Hogan's successor as chief counsel of General Motors. Behind him of course was Frederic Donner, chairman and chief executive. The latter's effective power in this matter would be qualified by members of the senior Finance Committee, where he sat with the ambivalent Mr. Sloan, the observer and critic Bradley, and others who were still there from the distant past.

Brownell's original advice to Time Inc. not to do anything at present was logical, since if they fired me while my case against General Motors was on, they could expect me to sue them for complicity with General Motors in the suppression of the book. The consequence of his intervention combined the prospect of the loss of the book with the loss of my job at *Fortune,* and damage to my ability to make a living in the publishing business. In effect, he put these stakes together in the form of a threat to my position in the fields of writing and publishing. So the need to win, in some sense of winning, became imperative, and the more things piled up, the more determined I had to be about it. But how, when the other side said they believed that in my winning the book they would lose General Motors? If they believed that or, in any case, if their chief counsel held fast to his requirement that the outside lawyers, Cravath, and the layman powers inside General Motors must act on that assumption, they could be intransigent below the level of reason. So it seemed on the part of their lawyers in late July.

The aggressive actions of Cravath for General Motors and Brownell for Time Inc., on the same day after four coterminous months, gave General Motors an advantage. It made them appear strong and me relatively weak. They indicated they were willing to contest the issue in court while putting front and side pressure on me and my team to face the consequences if I did not drop the suit—which might explain General Motors' long neglect of our standing offer to negotiate. This had the look of what is known in poker as a position play, one that favors

bluffing opponents who appear weak. The visibility of the position compromises it. Whatever their hand, logically, they
should bet. But we didn't feel weak, despite Brownell's threatening judgments, and we didn't think General Motors was all
that strong. So we called their bluff, as we read it, and went
ahead with them toward court: a bit of the game of chicken for
both sides. The strain of the countdown was such that one
would think that something should give . . . and it did.

On September 6, eleven days after Ennis served the summons
on General Motors, he received a statement from General Motors that took them into a one-hundred-eighty-degree turn
away from the direction of imminent confrontation in court.

They wanted to talk about the book. Eddie called me. He
said that General Motors had prepared a revised version of the
book and would have no objection to its being published. Their
"statement" quoted from my contract with Mr. Sloan that he
could publish or not publish. But, they said, Mr. Sloan wanted
my assistance in updating the revised book and seeing it
through publication. This would take substantial time, for
which Mr. Sloan would pay. If I accepted, I would be expected
to dismiss the suit against General Motors.

Eddie talked to Barnum at Cravath. He learned that Mr.
Sloan, who had not seen the revised book, had asked whether
my name was on it. A cautionary question. "Mr. Sloan is very
fond of John McDonald," Barnum said. Mr. Sloan wanted to
be sure I came along. He also said for General Motors' side
that Mr. Sloan would not approve anything that was objection-
able to them. That put the legal matter of Sloan's text between
General Motors and myself.

Ennis told Barnum that I would meet with Sloan, and both
lawyers were pleased at the prospect of a cooperative solution
instead of overt litigation; they expressed this in such words as

"fine," "dispose of case," "let it rest." Eddie said he hoped I would approve the revisions. If they were not acceptable, we had a difficult problem. He cautioned me to get all the information possible, and not to break off at the first sign of a bad revision; to withhold opinion; to get the story of what happened. Meanwhile he would keep the suit pending. All this I made note of while on the telephone with Ennis on September 6, 1962.

Revisions from General Motors, while probably raising horrendous editorial problems, could for the first time reveal something about the mystery of their objections to the book. The proposal to meet, apparently coming from General Motors' headquarters, along with Mr. Sloan's request to bring me in to review the revisions, would bring the principal parties together around the book in a sort of negotiation. This proposal also had the side effect of dispelling the invidious fictions created by Moore, supported by Bromley, and adopted by Brownell for Time Inc. That sideshow was finished.

On September 20, two weeks later, I had a note from Catharine Stevens, who wrote that there were signs that Mr. Sloan was preparing for this new phase in the life of the book. She had heard that he had spoken to the Sloan Foundation, where, by her choice, she was now working, about borrowing her to work with him on the book. She perked up at this, though the information as she received it was not entirely clear. She wrote:

... Anyway, Alfred [She was his only contemporary to call him that, and then only when speaking about him] is arranging things to GO, GO, GO, apparently. Have you seen him yet? He's very deaf now and can hardly hear anything. At the luncheon [the Foundation's, held that day] he asked me to sit next to him, and I wrote notes to let him know what the others were talking about so he could chime in. It's not very much news, but I thought you'd like to know. I'll "flash" if there's anything more. [In a footnote, she added: "I'll bet Alfred is glad you brought that suit. The book would never ever have been considered for publication without it."]

After a month of discussions on how to get together, Cravath and my lawyers arranged a meeting of General Motors, Mr. Sloan, me—and the lawyers; it was to be held on October 3, 1962 in the conference room of Mr. Sloan's office. It would become a "summit" meeting of the major players in the conflict.

## October–December 1962

The atmosphere of the meeting in Sloan's conference room was formal yet amicable, fitting for a first armistice. As we convened around a rectangular table, Bruce "Judge" Bromley, bright and cheerful, seated himself at the head. Mr. Sloan was composed and reserved on this first occasion of our meeting since the suit had begun. He sat to the right of the "Judge" and I sat to his left, across from Mr. Sloan. To Mr. Sloan's right sat Tex Moore, whose demeanor was a model of nonaggression. Moore was making his first show in the case since Time Inc.'s intervention and since Brownell had been brought in to sub for him. On around the table were John Barnum, assigned to the case by Cravath; Al Powers, chief counsel of General Motors; Franklin La Rowe, from General Motors headquarters, designated by General Motors to work with Mr. Sloan and me; George A. Brooks, secretary of the General Motors Corporation, representing its chief executive Frederic Donner; and next to me on my left my lawyer, Bert Mayers. Nine altogether, with Brooks, La Rowe, and Powers coming directly from General Motors. As Mr. Sloan's lawyer, Moore was made chairman of the meeting.

When all were seated and it was time to open the meeting, Mr. Sloan came out of his reverie, reached out and slammed the palm of his hand down on a copy of our original manuscript

lying on the table in front of him and said: "It's a masterpiece."
It was a stunning strategic gesture on his part, making clear to
everyone at the table that this was a manuscript that he had
the highest regard for, and that he would not tolerate frivolous
revisions. I broke the ice by referring to the "Judge" as my
counsel, which got a laugh from him and lent an amiable tone
to the meeting.

Al Powers said he had thought up the idea of the revision
and publication and had taken it up with Donner. He said
changes occur where there are documents in the book; he also
said that the documents belonged to GM—a dubious claim,
later renounced. Concerning accuracy changes, I said that in
1959 the book had been checked by GM and its accuracy approved, and that we had also had an outside review of some
of the chapters.

I said that the memorandum on General Motors' proposal
before us, dated September 21, had been given to me late yesterday, October 2, and neither I nor my counsel had had time to
study it properly. Thus we could not now go into details, which
were not relevant anyway before I had seen their revisions to
the book. Bert Mayers also made this point, saying that we did
not accept their memorandum as a whole.

The memorandum, apparently drafted by lawyers for General Motors, stated what the top executives of General Motors
had in mind for revising the book, and was the subject of the
meeting:

MEMORANDUM FOR ACTION WITH RESPECT TO THE GENERAL
MOTORS STORY

1. Mr. Sloan has before him a suggested revision of the original *General Motors Story* which General Motors has stated would be acceptable to it for publication, subject to final check as to accuracy and
bringing certain parts of the story down to date. General Motors has

stated that of course it is up to Mr. Sloan as to whether the revisions are acceptable and as to whether or not the book shall be published.

2. Mr. Sloan has accepted the idea of publication of the book incorporating the suggested revisions, subject to such further revision in the interest of literary style and accuracy as he shall finally approve and as shall be acceptable to General Motors.

3. In order to get the book in final form for publication as soon as possible, Mr. Sloan desires the assistance of Mr. McDonald and asks that Mr. McDonald devote such time as will be necessary to complete the book. Mr. Sloan fixes as a target that the first volume shall be completed and released for publication within a period of four months and the second volume by the end of a period of six months from the beginning of the work on the revised volumes.

4. It is assumed that Mr. McDonald will either get a leave of absence from *Fortune* for the required period or be relieved from his duties there sufficiently to enable him to perform his part in the completion of the book. If it is necessary for *Fortune* to give Mr. McDonald a leave of absence without pay, Mr. Sloan will reimburse Mr. McDonald for any resulting loss in compensation.

5. It is agreed that the work will start not on the original volumes, but on the revised volumes now in the hands of Mr. Sloan.

6. General Motors has designated Mr. Franklin La Rowe, who is in the General Motors office in New York, as the one to work with Mr. Sloan and Mr. McDonald on the completion of the book. Mr. La Rowe will be responsible for those phases of the work which involve checking for accuracy, the bringing down to date of those parts of the story that may require it, and for the consideration of further revisions of the book from the standpoint of General Motors.

7. Mr. Sloan will execute an agreement for the publication of the book with Doubleday or, if Doubleday should not wish to do it, with another publisher with equal standing, in such form as he and his counsel shall determine appropriate.

In summary, starting with the revised volumes now in Mr. Sloan's hands and assuming as he does that the further work of the book will result in a final revision satisfactory to him and to General Motors, Mr. Sloan has decided to proceed with the publication of the book.

After we had got through with the memorandum for the time being, Moore asked if I could be detached from *Fortune* immediately. I explained that I was doing a story for the December issue and the question of when I would be available, if we found a basis for going ahead, would be one that I would have to put to the managing editor. I said that I too of course wanted to publish. I would have to see what happened to the book in the revised version.

The General Motors representatives said that no copy of the revised book was in the room. Mr. Sloan had one copy, which he had taken home, and Powers said that he had a copy in Detroit. Mr. Sloan mentioned that he had a list of the revisions, and inquired whether they were complete. There was some confusion in which Powers and others said the list that Mr. Sloan referred to was not a complete list, but a list of additional revisions that GM wanted over and above their revised version of the book.

Mr. Sloan said he would have the book and the list sent over to my office that afternoon.

The meeting broke up. I returned to my office at *Fortune,* and told Dan Seligman about it—he was my editor on the story on which I was starting to work. Dan proposed to the acting managing editor, Max Ways, that time off be arranged for me to study the revision and discuss it with Mr. Sloan. Ways refused, saying *Fortune* should be "neutral," a novel posture for Time Inc. in this affair. Mr. Sloan sent his copy of the revised book over to me and I began reading it that night.

Under the rule of the lawyers, Mr. Sloan and I were not entirely free to meet. But because of her position, Catharine could see and talk to each of us and was a go-between when we had something to say to each other, as in these notes of hers the day after the October 3 meeting:

I went in to see Mr. Sloan about not being able to take the courses I had planned to take for doctorate study since working on the book meant a 7-day week with no time for study. So I'll take an afternoon and get out of these things. I said that John had called me about the book.

Mr. Sloan: Yes, he asked me if it was all right. I just wanted to tell you about it first. John said he (would) read it last night. I don't know whether or not he did.

CS: He's reading it and comparing it with the other book.

Mr. Sloan: (Who didn't hear all of this.) We're going to work with the new book. We're going to call the book the new book. I delivered a copy of the new book to John yesterday afternoon. We're going to work with the new one now. I'm going to suggest a change in the name—I'll tell John—instead of *The General Motors Story—The Evolution of General Motors.*

Catharine wrote him on a slip of paper (writing, because of his deafness): "John wanted me to tell you that he started to read the new book and will continue tonight and on the weekend. It's a lengthy job, as you know." Mr. Sloan said it was OK, and something like, We won't get started anyway until John has read the book.

About a week later, anxious about my reading, Mr. Sloan inquired again through Catharine, and she replied on my behalf.

I gave John your message yesterday. He asked me tell you that he had been reading the "new" book evenings and on the weekend, but it was too long to finish and get an accurate impression of in that time.

He now has to write the *Fortune* story. That is going to occupy the next three weeks, round-the-clock. John regrets this very much as he is eager to complete his reading of the "new book," but *Fortune* is not giving him any relief.

John told them about the situation here, but the Managing Editor has not released John from the story (American Smelting ASARCO that John was on, but had not started to write, when this happened). So John is not able to continue reading the "new book" as he has that imperative obligation from which he is not being relieved. The obstacle is his *Fortune* work—for the next few weeks.

Mr. Sloan took the note and read it carefully. "That's awful bad," he said. Then he read it again. He asked me: "Did you get the key [i.e., to the office files of the book]?"

"Yes."

Then he looked at the note again and said: "John can't help it. I tell you what we had better do. As soon as he finishes the first book, have him send it to me. I haven't any copy. I was told I was going to get an extra copy, but I haven't received it. So I'll get the copy from John as soon as he finishes the first book so I can read it. Or if he's not working on it and can't finish it, ask him to send it to me."

Then I told him I was going to the Foundation Scholarship luncheon but that I'd worked for him last night. He said that I didn't have to be so particular—that was all right. Later Mr. Sloan asked, Do I understand that after John has finished the story on American Smelting, he will be able to get on the book? Will he be able to get released from *Fortune* after he finishes that story? Will you ask John the next time you see him?

I read through endless changes in the revision—made without apparent rhyme or reason, and showing no pattern. I then turned the book back to Catharine for her consideration. She made point-by-point comparisons of revision and original, and we discussed what was happening to the book. On November 9, I went to discuss the matter with Mr. Sloan, and to give him the detailed report of our first observations that I had prepared. When I asked him whether he had read the book as revised by GM, he said he had not, and added that he was afraid he would get upset. He had decided to let me read it and tell him about it. Here is the text as I handed it to him.

Report to Alfred P. Sloan, Jr.

The revised book is a large task, on the order of 1,000 pages.

Until last week I have had no free time from *Fortune*.

Thanks to much preparatory work by Catharine, I have been able to review Volume I, but not to do more than leaf through Volume II on a selective basis, studying the changes. It is not realistic to speak of it as a "new book." It is our book altered. Necessarily I have had to work from our book to evaluate what they have done. There are a vast number of revisions of our book and the materials it is based on; about two of every three pages in Volume I have some alterations varying from single words to the entire contents of several pages in a row.

Much has been rewritten and there are numerous additions and omissions. So there is a lot to study and my conclusions are not complete. I can't give you a chapter and verse report today; it will take some time to spell it out to you in terms of the text. In fact, it is a very big job to do just that. But let me make a few observations.

1) The largest set of changes is aimed at your original texts. Quotes, sources, and dates of your old memos, reports, etc. have been removed and the texts have been changed from the present tense (of, say, 1920 or other date) to the past tense as if they were written in 1962. These Sloan texts themselves have also been revised, with additions, omissions, and rewritings. Most of these texts were prepared by you in [between] 1918 and 1927 on the subjects of organization policy, Product Policy, and financial policy. They constitute a set of business concepts which were carried into action and embodied in the development of General Motors, transforming [it] from the loose organization of Durant's time into the great corporation of today. The interaction between these ideas and the events described in the book is what made General Motors dynamic and by the same token that interaction is what makes our book interesting. As your ideas were written over a period of time in relation to events, they represent a history of basic business ideas, original then though now some of them are common as they have spread throughout business. Your remarkable foresight in the history of the automobile business and your general teaching of business concepts have been the most striking thing about the book in the comments of outstanding historians, editors, and businessmen to whom we showed the manuscript. . . .

Your business papers written long ago are a distinguished piece of operational writing. You were a writer, a rare thing in business. In their primary form they are the core of what the publisher called "The Federalist Papers of American Business," when he and his editors first saw our book. A serious effect of the revisions is to downgrade your role in the development of the Corporation and your contributions to American business.

2) The loss of time, quotes, and dates alone (apart from the revisions of the texts) is enormous. It changes the angle of vision from a position before the events which they were to bring about or influence, to a position after the events, as if written from the armchair forty years later. Thus your foresight has become hindsight, your originality has become mediocrity. Who is going to believe that this massive book,

built out of the materials of a lifetime of work, was written, as the revised book misleadingly states, equally from your memory and the record? In that pretense there is a loss of credibility. The great thing about our book is its solid foundations open to the eyes of the reader and its unchallengable integrity. There is no kidding about it as there was no kidding in the way you and Mr. Pratt and Mr. Brown and the Du Ponts built the modern General Motors Corporation. The revised book is a different kind of book. It does not even sound like you.

3) The book contains other original texts from which have been removed quotes, sources, and dates. Part of the content of these has been revised, part remains. What remains, not written by you, appears now as if it were written by you. For example, passages from the 1920 Annual Report of the Corporation, and the words of Donaldson Brown, John Pratt, and others, with revisions in their content, now appear as your writing in 1962. So we have lost the original references and the integrity too.

4) The rest of the book, developed by us between 1954 and 1959, has also been revised with changes in both form and content.

5) Very few of the changes are aimed at clarifying and improving the book. Most of them have an opposite effect. The revised book contains a large number of inaccuracies, deflected meanings, misleading statements, and some statements without any meaning. As it stands, I am sorry to say this book has lost validity, quality, credibility, and flavor. I am not concluding that there is no hope but as it stands you could not properly give your good name to the revised book. It would harm your reputation both as to the realities of your business career and to your role as an author. The same of course goes for me.

I want to finish Volume II and discuss with you the changes in substance in both volumes and an evaluation of our problem.

As he read this report, it was obvious that he was dismayed at the severity of my criticism. At one point he said: "I am upset." Another time, commenting to himself, he said: "This is awful." When he had finished he said that in view of my report he could not accept General Motors' revision. He said, "It's your reputation and mine." He said that he and I and Catharine Stevens should get together and compare our book with theirs, put what we want in, making a new revision and present it to General Motors for their approval. "So first," he said, "we must arrange your leave of absence from *Fortune.*" He mentioned this question of leave several times; it was the paramount operative point he had to make. He said at one juncture that there was something he wanted me to understand: that he had nothing to do with the revision; did not know they were doing it, did not participate in it, and learned of it for the first time when Tex Moore walked into his office and handed him the revision. "I was flabbergasted," he said.

On my leaving, he urged me again to come over. He said he did not think he would live long and he said he was not as good as he used to be, that he was not as strong and that his memory was poor; that he was good for stretches of time. He said that he had disposed of all his affairs, including the management of the Foundation, and had nothing important left to do before he died but to get this book out. He said again that we should do a second revision and added, "I will fight General Motors for the things you want." I made no commitment but said I would see him again in about a week.

Two days later I wrote, for my lawyers, some strategical observations on Mr. Sloan, General Motors, the revised book, and *Fortune:*

November 11, 1962
Some observations after seeing Mr. Sloan last Friday.

Sloan struck me as sincere in his desire to find a compromise and get out the book. His urgency is obviously justified by his age, his desire for the book, and the immediate value it has for him in making life interesting. Yet I have also the feeling that he was carrying out an instruction to get me on leave from *Fortune* and working for him. The two motives are not contradictory. GM-Cravath may have their own reasons for putting me and our litigation on ice for a while. Eddie suggested to me the possibility that if they are not acting in good faith, they may have in mind to prolong the editorial operation until he dies;

also my leave from *Fortune* has danger there. I might not get back. These points need to be considered.

About *Fortune*. There is the possibility, even the likelihood, that my future there is not bright, no matter what I do. They raised the question of my professional reputation, and while GM and Sloan have washed them out on that, Time Inc. has not yet retracted it. A break like that in an organization is hard to heal. It may be that I must hold GM responsible for that insecurity; in just what way I don't know. I should think, however, that on a leave of absence for six months, they could hardly block my return without getting themselves into more trouble than they rationally should care to entertain. . . .

In my letter, I discussed several courses of action and reached a decision to request a leave of absence from *Fortune* in order to work with Mr. Sloan on revising the book in an attempt to reach an agreement with GM. Not knowing GM's resistance points, I could not forecast how long this would take. And even assuming that GM would yield on the basic necessities of the book, I did not know if it would be as good as it had been. But I supposed that those were the fortunes of war. I could try.

Catharine was as excited as Mr. Sloan was by the new prospect, though typically more skeptical. We got a copy of the revision to Al Chandler to review. On November 12 I talked to Al about it on the telephone, and on November 20 he wrote me a letter containing substantial point-by-point comparisons of the two texts, which gave us outside confirmation of our observations on the wide gap between the original and General Motors' revision.

Alarmed by my pessimistic report on the revision, Bert, Bill, and Eddie held a conference about an impending impasse with General Motors just when their top management had made an apparent attempt at reconciling the conflict. They thought that I was required to make a try at closing the gap by working with Mr. Sloan as General Motors had proposed. As it was both sides were agreed that Mr. Sloan and I should meet to work,

with just one legal problem to resolve: an agreement in writing
between the lawyers, a "stipulation" of the conditions for such
work while the lawsuit remained pending.

On November 20, 1962 Ennis sent me a letter concerning
my legal position on the revised manuscript:

... As a result of your memo November 11th and our discussion with
Bert and Bill yesterday it seems to me that you are not in a position
to refuse to work on the revisions because of doubt of GM's approval
of a satisfactory text (which I doubt) but you are pretty much forced
to go through the extensive revision discussions and the only question
is what conditions should be placed upon your doing so.

1. The minimum is the proposed stipulation that the revision discussions shall be treated like negotiations for settlement and not referred
to in any subsequent trial. Of course such a stipulation cuts two ways
because one can never clearly predict which side will be helped at a
trial by proof of prior settlement negotiations and its implicit admis-
sions. On the balance the safer course seems to be to require a stipulation. The difficult question is to determine what else to require.

2. It is not practical to ask Sloan to agree now to publish without
GM's approval if GM is unreasonable in the revision discussions.
There is no chance of getting him to publish without GM's approval
in view of all the GM influence surrounding him. Nor do I think it
possible to get him to agree now to place the book in trust to be published hereafter if he concludes GM is unreasonable.

3. The only practical alternative is to try to fix your economic interest
in the book as a condition of your working on the revisions. You could
say to Sloan that you are willing to spend the time working on the
revisions in the hope that you can get the book published but that you
honestly do not believe that GM will agree to a book to which Sloan
and you are willing to affix your names so that at the end of three or
six months you will find yourself just where you are with a mere delay
in your action against GM. In view of the time which you have already
spent away from *Fortune,* to the detriment of your advancement as
an editor, you should not be asked to spend additional time without
the real prospect of a favorable result [and] without some protection.
In the light of your pending suit the only possible protection is the
placing of an agreed value on your interest in the book with the provision that if a publishing contract is not entered into within six months

on a book with which you are willing to be associated as an editor you will be paid the agreed sum, dismiss your action, and have no further rights or action in the book.

To this proposal the objection may be made that with a large sum coming you will have no interest in working out the revisions into a book you are willing to sign. On the contrary, you much prefer to have your years of work published and to obtain your remuneration from the book rather than a sum of money in lieu of publication. As an established editor you can assert very convincingly that you prefer publication plus its economic rewards in place of a sum of money and elimination of yourself from the book.

4. There remains negotiating a deposit of the book in trust for later publication. I think it better for you not to get into this. If you do you will not be paid your economic interest if the book is to be subsequently published. Moreover, GM will not be satisfied by a five or ten year delay in publication if, as I believe, they are against publication. The only reason for bringing in a deposit of the book in trust is to indicate to Sloan that you are not abandoning him and the book if you are paid off but are also fighting for later publication. But what interest has he really shown in publication after his death? And if such publication is arranged it will cut down any present payment of your economic interest. I think you should leave it alone and let the Columbia School of Business, which has shown an interest, push that proposal. . . .

In addition to this letter, Eddie also sent me, on the same day, another one. This letter was formal, more conclusive, representing apparently for the record the collective view of my lawyers. It was also briefer and more pessimistic in tone and outlook, omitting entirely the possibility of my negotiating the survival of the original book in some kind of trust over time. It was dated November 20, 1962.

. . . I refer to your report to me of your recent discussion with Mr. Sloan and the proposal that you request a leave of absence from *Fortune* for at least three months to work with him on the proposed revisions of "The General Motors Story" suggested by General Motors. You have requested my opinion whether this proposed procedure will in any way prejudice your legal rights in this pending action.

The complaint alleges that the defendant without justification has suppressed publication of the book which it had previously authorized and that this constitutes a tortuous interference with your property rights in the book. Adoption of the proposed procedure to examine in detail the defendant's present objections to the book conceivably could be construed as implying some recognition on your part of the defendant's legal right to propose changes in the book, which of course by this action you deny. I believe that such action on your part would merely indicate your willingness to mitigate the damage caused you by the defendant in seeking to remove the basis for its suppression of the book. There is some unavoidable risk in undertaking to discuss at length with the defendant its proposed revisions of the book which you claim it has no right to suppress. If you do go ahead with the proposal to obtain withdrawal of the defendant's opposition to the book I recommend as a minimum a stipulation in the pending action stating that the discussion of revisions shall be treated as negotiations for settlement of the case which are not to prejudice the rights of the parties or to be introduced into evidence or referred to in any subsequent trial of the action.

The only course which occurs to me beyond the imperfect protection of a stipulation is an agreement with the defendant fixing at this time the economic value of your interest in the book and providing that if discussion of the proposed revisions does not result in a contract within six months to publish the book in a form to which you are willing to lend your name you will then be paid the value of your interest in settlement of this action and have no further interest in the publication of the book. . . .

This hard line on settlement reflected the discontent felt at Fitelson and Mayers, particularly by Bert, who had at one time got the notion (certainly mistaken) that the Du Ponts—with some residual influence—were behind the suppression and General Motors in any case would never yield on the publication or survival of the original book. The logic of this view— that we were unlikely to get a settlement by publication—was not a happy one for Eddie, whose interest in the case had always involved a sense of historical public interest in the accomplished book. As for me, in strictly legal matters I deferred to my lawyers, and they had done more than very well, I thought, in meeting the Brownell/Time Inc. diversion and bringing General Motors into a kind of negotiating arena. But when it came to the substantive matter of negotiating, I insisted on a policy of including the survival of the book in the negotiations.

My lawyers were my very good friends, Bill across four decades—it was always with a feeling of pleasure that I entered their offices—so these tensions were personally felt. They were built unavoidably into the nature of the case, the only advisable legal recourse available to lift the suppression being to sue for damages. My view was not to push my lawyers into interminable legal work out of sentiment or principle at any cost (mainly their cost, to the advantage of General Motors); my view was that standing for the survival of the book, while a matter of professional desire and attitude, was also strategic, based on the common interest that Mr. Sloan and I had in the book, and the implicit alliance that followed from it. He had had on his own little usable strength when General Motors put down the book, threatening him with responsibility for publishing something that would "destroy General Motors." That was the lock that the General Motors lawyers had on him. Not until I sued was it possible for Mr. Sloan to move into his characteristic middle ground. He had brought our tacit alliance into the open on being told of the General Motors revision when he asked if my name was on it. Although his power and influence in General Motors were diminished by his age and retirement from nearly all active participation in the corporation, no one in General Motors wanted to cross him with more than legal abstractions. So our alliance was important on several counts and I could maintain it by standing on my own for the publication of a valid book, and to the extent possible, negotiating its survival. My lawyers were persuaded to agree with this policy.

If I was in a tough spot trying to move General Motors, they too were in a tough spot, holding out for what Mr. Sloan, contrary to his hopes, now realized was an editorially and historically invalid revision. In the conflict between the original and the revision, we would have to see what would happen. Meanwhile there could be no meeting sanctioned by the lawyers until the issue of the stipulation of the conditions of meeting was resolved. In the legal presumption that a lot was at stake in the writing of the stipulation, the lawyers, Barnum for General Motors, Eddie for me, began with civility a battle of stipulations.

Eddie led off with the following draft which he sent to Barnum at Cravath on November 29, 1962. The following is a facsimile of our first proposal to General Motors:

SUPREME COURT OF THE STATE OF NEW YORK
       COUNTY OF NEW YORK

| JOHN McDONALD | | |
|---|---|---|
| Plaintiff | \| | |
| 《 》 vs. | \| | STIPULATION |
| GENERAL MOTORS CORPORATION | \| | |
| Defendant | \| | |

WHEREAS, it is alleged in the complaint that the defendant suppressed publication of the book called "The General Motors Story" prepared by Alfred P. Sloan, Jr. and the plaintiff, and

WHEREAS, defendant has proposed to plaintiff that plaintiff obtain a leave of absence from his employer for a period of from three to six months and work with Alfred P. Sloan, Jr. on a revised version of the book prepared by defendant with the objective of producing a version of the book satisfactory to Alfred P. Sloan, Jr., plaintiff and defendant, it is hereby

STIPULATED AND AGREED by and between plaintiff and defendant through their attorneys that plaintiff's proposed activities in respect of the said revised version of the book shall be without prejudice to the contention of either party in this action and shall be treated as settlement negotiations and not introduced into evidence or other wise referred to in any subsequent trial or other prosecution of this action.

With a certain amount of rigmarole General Motors responded to this stipulation, which was understandable as their lawyers were feeling their way, it seems, without a specific objective except to get me to drop the lawsuit. They would not commit General Motors to any publishing decision of Mr. Sloan's, nor of course would I—a most peculiar situation for an author.

Barnum conveyed their thoughts to Eddie, who wrote to me on December 5 laying out the General Motors offer.

. . . Mr. Barnum, for Judge Bromley, advises me that General Motors is agreeable to the principle that all of our discussions to date and your proposed work on revisions are without prejudice to the positions of the parties. But stating this in a stipulation leaves General Motors in the position that at the end of the revision work you may decide whether or not the final product is a satisfactory substitute for the law suit and, if you don't agree, retain your rights under the law suit and perhaps also retain your contractual rights in the proceeds of the book which you do not wholly accept.

Mr. Barnum suggested, and I of course rejected, the thought that you might be willing to state now that the General Motors revised book subject to any changes you persuade them to make is satisfactory and upon publication the law suit will be dismissed.

I told him that all you were prepared to say was that the revised book is not satisfactory but you had sufficient hope that something could be worked out and you were willing to try for several months.

I also rejected the thought that you would be willing to submit to General Motors now a list of the further revisions you wanted as impractical as a basis for some present determination of what was to be published. In the conversation it was also brought out that General Motors present revisions are not final and it reserves the right to update the book, etc.

Finally, looking for neutral ground, the question arose whether both you and General Motors would accept the decision of Mr. Sloan to publish as disposing of the law suit. I said my view was that Mr. Sloan might be so anxious to publish the book in his lifetime that he would agree to [General] Motors' revisions, to which you as editor would not lend your name and that such a book and your profits there from would not be a satisfactory substitute for the law suit. Mr. Barnum would not say that General Motors was prepared to accept Mr. Sloan's decisions on the final form of the book but we agreed we could explore the matter with our clients. That is where the matter stands.

My view is that our position that you are willing to work on the revisions without prejudice is all we can do and you cannot now commit yourself to dismiss the law suit if Sloan agrees to publish a book not acceptable to you. I think the defendant would be reasonable in asking you to agree to dismiss if a book agreeable to you is published and thus remit to you your profits from the book without compensating you for the delay in publication. But General Motors cannot reasonably ask the additional step that you agree to dismiss your law suit if a book not satisfactory to you is published. . . .

Not knowing what Mr. Sloan might be hearing from the other side, I dropped in to see him on December 14, and sent a report on the meeting to my lawyers, which consisted of the message on typed cards I had handed him because he was hard of hearing:

Mr. Sloan,

I have been ready to come over here and get started working with you since I completed the *Fortune* story last week. I have been held up by some sort of technicality down at Cravath. My counsel made a routine request for a stipulation that my work with you in the next few months be understood to be without prejudice to my position. Cravath has a problem about it. As soon as they clear this up, I'll be right over to make arrangements with you, and with *Fortune* for a leave.

Of course the time has not been all lost. Catharine has done a lot of preparatory work that we would have to do in any case. I have been over much of this with her and we have developed a fairly good picture of the editorial and other problems of the book.

But the danger is that if Cravath-GM do not clear the way soon, I shall be entangled in another *Fortune* story for two or three months. A new big story (the Martin-Marietta Corp.) is looming up. In fact, I have already been assigned to it and in another week I'll be into it.

I came in to see you today to let you know that I am as eager as I know you are to get started on a constructive approach to the book.

In our discussion, Mr. Sloan appeared not to understand the stipulation matter, and I did not go into it further. He said, however, that whatever the difficulty was, he would ask Tex Moore to get it cleared up right away. The rest of our talk was rather general, what method of work we might pursue, and so on. He was very cordial and anxious to get some action.

Eddie continued to negotiate with Barnum, attempting to reach a stipulation satisfactory to both sides. Eddie felt as if he had gotten into a tangle of Catch-22s and had become wary of a trap, as he reported to me on December 18:

> . . . I advised you that Barnum indicated that GM was not agreeable to a proposed stipulation to work on the book revisions without prejudice to the law suit without adding that upon Mr. Sloan's publication of some version of the book, with or without your approval, you would dismiss the law suit. GM argues that if Sloan publishes there is no suppression and that Sloan as author has reserved the right to publish any version he chooses. We were not prepared in advance to stipulate dismissal of the suit upon Sloan's publication of a version not approved by you.
>
> Upon further discussion, however, we felt GM might exploit with Sloan your refusal to be bound by his decision although there was no clear indication that GM was willing to be bound by his decision, including his decision to publish the original version approved by you but not by GM. Therefore, I called Barnum back and asked him whether GM would agree to be bound by Sloan's decision to publish the original version without any of the GM revisions. He said GM would agree if you would and that Tex Moore would inquire from Sloan whether this formula would be agreeable to Sloan, namely, that the parties would stipulate to accept his decision on the book to be published and if a book were published by Sloan the suit would be dismissed. Sloan's attitude is now being explored and you may wish to talk to Sloan about it also before any such agreement is made.
>
> Superficially, it seems fair that the two parties, contending for different versions of the book and with equal access to the author, should

accept the author's decision. But this is true only if Sloan states that he will publish whether or not you or GM approves. Sloan could publish the original version over any objection by GM and chose not to do so only over loyalty to GM. Even though GM stipulates no objection to a version chosen by Sloan will he in fact be willing to publish anything objected to by GM? If he will not the proposed stipulation is illusory in that if he publishes a version not approved by you your law suit is dismissed but in no case may he be willing to publish a version not approved by GM. This, however, would leave you with your law suit.

We must consider also whether such a stipulation would be a trap in another sense, namely, evidence that GM was no longer suppressing the book because it agreed to publication of any version chosen by Sloan even though GM's refusal to approve any version would effectively suppress the book if Sloan would not publish without GM's approval.

On the one hand we must avoid being maneuvered by GM into the position of appearing to refuse to accept Sloan's judgment by refusing to stipulate dismissal upon publication by Sloan. On the other hand we must avoid a stipulation to accept Sloan's judgment which binds you to dismiss the suit on publication of a book you do not like but only in form equally binds GM to accept a version it does not like because of a private understanding that Sloan will not publish anything that GM does not like. I don't know how we are going to get the necessary assurance from Sloan (1) that he will treat such a stipulation as a binding withdrawal by GM of any objection to a version he decides to publish, including the first version approved by him and (2) that he will promptly determine the version to be published. . . .

Three days after Christmas I went to see Mr. Sloan again, in his office. This anomaly, wherein Mr. Sloan and I would meet while the lawyers debated the conditions under which they would allow us to meet, happened often, as it did here and at times in communication through Catharine Stevens. Like the lawyers, we were both interested in getting a simple stipulation that would allow us to work together without harm to the legal position of either side. As usual, because of his difficulty in hearing, I typed on cards:

The lawyers are having some difficulty arranging the stipulation under which you and I should work. As I understand it, Cravath-GM are concerned about the situation that would arise if you were to publish a GM-revised book which did not meet my standards and so did not have my approval and did not carry my name. There has also been some talk to the effect that Cravath was going to have Mr. Moore speak to you about your publishing a book with or without GM's consent. I don't know what kind of reality this line of thought could have. Do you?

If agreement on the conditions of our work is not reached in a few days I shall be so involved in a new *Fortune* story that it may be another three months before I can get back here with you. I am concerned about that.

Mr. Sloan replied, "Your standards are my standards," that is, for whatever it is worth, he said in effect he would not publish a book of which I did not approve. Obviously that did not imply that he would publish a book of which GM did not approve. He asked me if I thought it practical to try to get a valid book in view of the revisions GM had requested. I wrote my answer in longhand (and later telephoned it in) as follows:

I don't know how we can find out if there is a book they would not object to and that is also valid except by working together for three months or so, as has been suggested. Maybe then the specific problems would become clear, and the general question whether there is an irreconcilability would also become clear.

In the discussion I also said again that the present GM revision was not a valid book.

Mr. Sloan showed me a telephone message from Mr. Moore of an earlier date, after our previous meeting, which said that my lawyers were making difficulties which he would try to clear up in a couple of days. Mr. Sloan said he would get hold of Mr. Moore and urge him again to hurry up with a stipulation. Again he proposed that he would write a letter to *Fortune,* with me present, and give it to me to deliver by hand.

On this occasion he asked for the cards. But I took them away, checked them with Eddie and then telephoned them in to his secretary.

On Monday, December 31, New Year's Eve, Mr. Sloan called me through his secretary and said he had arranged to see Mr. Moore Wednesday morning, January 2, and would get in touch with me immediately afterward.

## January–February 1963

With only one day off for New Year's of 1963, we resumed the match over a stipulation but were immediately interrupted to consider a question concerning Mr. Sloan's health. Given his age of eighty-eight, GM wanted to know what we should do if Mr. Sloan should become disabled or die with the issue of the book and the suit unresolved. Nothing had been said on this subject before except by Mr. Sloan privately at our meeting on November 9, where he had brought it up, saying his condition was not as good as it used to be and he did not expect to live long. His point was that it was urgent to arrange our meeting to work on the book. We should do so as soon as possible. My lawyers had wondered, perhaps suspected that Mr. Sloan's age was a factor in what appeared to them to be Cravath's delaying maneuvers around the stipulation. But the question came from their side; my records do not say explicitly who among them first brought it up. My guess is that it was Mr. Sloan himself. Given his earlier pessimistic confidence to me, it made sense for him to worry about the time it was taking to get a stipulation that would allow us to proceed.

Word on this matter came from Barnum to Eddie to me on January 3, 1963, in the form of a question: In view of Mr. Sloan's age, would I accept a proposal to designate a substitute for him if he should die or be disabled while the suit was still on; and, further, would I accept the designation of Albert Bradley as his substitute? Barnum reported an exchange between Moore and Mr. Sloan on the reaction they expected from me. Moore said, "McDonald will not be happy with that." Mr. Sloan disagreed: "No. McDonald would think Bradley the logical successor." Mr. Sloan was right. I preferred Bradley to Moore, even though Moore as Mr. Sloan's lawyer was supposed to represent Mr. Sloan's interest, and Bradley represented General Motors, an odd complex of reversals. Normally, Moore was in line to take over for Mr. Sloan. But Mr. Sloan, I think, had the insight or instinct to see that Moore with his multiple conflicts of interest and committed hostility to me would not well represent Mr. Sloan's real dilemma in my suit against General Motors, to which he was not a party except as a witness. Sloan and I were both guardians of the book, though each in a different way. With either of us out, the strength generated by our common ground was lost. Referring the question of a substitute to me was technically a courtesy but also a strategy, for Mr. Sloan could designate whomever he wished to represent him. Bradley was one of his oldest associates in General Motors, if not the oldest; he was present in 1919 and appears as assistant treasurer on the first organization chart of the corporation drawn up by the Pierre Du Pont group after their takeover in 1920. He thus knew the story in the book from his own experience. It was Bradley Mr. Sloan turned to when his wife died in 1956 to take his place as interim chairman of General Motors. When Mr. Sloan went abroad with his brother Raymond that year, he designated Bradley as the one I should deal with in his absence.

I had had occasion to write Bradley then about the engagement of Matson as our literary agent. When I called on him as expert consultant he played the game of approving the project's expanded budget in 1957. He kept his distance from Moore and separated himself from Moore's desire to destroy the project's files in 1959. Bradley had a round, amiable face and a ready smile and was casual and unpretentious. "There must be seventy men sitting on a roof," he said to me one day looking at some figures in his office. He meant that for some unknown reason they were not working, and his financial controls were good enough to pick up that fact. He had reviewed the chapter on General Motors' finances—his specialty—with me. He was cool. While others professed to fear that the publication of the book would cause the break-up of General Motors, Bradley wondered out loud to me just how they would reconstitute economies of scale among Pontiac, Oldsmobile, Buick, and Cadillac. Once my damage suit was on, he recognized it realistically. He wondered out loud in my presence why they all cared so much about the money, a mystery that would only deepen. In his genial and amused way, he was an unworried sophisticate. He could see the objective reality of Mr. Sloan's dilemma as well the General Motors interest. Hence it seemed to me, as it did to Mr. Sloan, that he would be the logical substitute if anything happened to Mr. Sloan. I could imagine a negotiation with him for the survival of the book. My lawyers felt differently. They thought that the death or disablement of Mr. Sloan would be bad for me, and that the book would die with him. I don't recall any formal agreement with General Motors in the matter of succession and of course they didn't need one. The idea of designating Bradley as substitute for Mr. Sloan made Bradley a shadow player in the present and extended Mr. Sloan's reach beyond the grave.

I can't say it was Mr. Sloan's urgency that moved General Motors but he was now in the center of some strong action. As

promised, he called in Moore on January 2 and that afternoon
through his secretary telephoned me a message:

Mr. Sloan states that he had a lengthy conference with Mr. Moore this
morning and the proposal for the stipulation that Mr. Moore made
to Mr. Sloan was satisfactory to him and he is willing to accept same.
He understands that it has also been gone over with Mr. McDonald
and is satisfactory to him. Mr. Moore said he would get his people
immediately in touch with Mr. McDonald's counsel so that the stipulation could be put in concrete form. It must also be approved by General
Motors but Mr. Moore thought there would be no question about
that. If all this is correct then we can start. Mr. Moore states that after
my counsel had gone over the matter with you, if everything is according to this memorandum, it would be in order for you to make
an application to *Fortune* for a leave of absence to review and finalize
the book for publication. Mr. Moore thought this should be done by
you and I would suggest we get busy on it right away as it might take
some little time. Now you told me that if we did not have the stipulation finalized this week you would have to take another important
assignment which would delay work on the book for three months. I
can appreciate that might well be so. Mr. Moore thought we could
get it done without delay in view that everyone seems to agree. Anyway
he will do the best he can and that is the reason why I suggest that
you take it up with *Fortune* so there will be no delay at that end. I am
very well satisfied with that step if you are and you know perfectly
well that I will carry out my part to the best advantage of making the
book as interesting and valuable as I can.

I said I did not want to have any misunderstandings with Mr.
Sloan and asked his secretary to convey him the following: "I
express satisfaction only with the stipulation proposed by my
counsel to the effect that everything be let rest while Mr. Sloan
and I went to work." Eddie and I discussed this exchange. Apart
from the dangers in the forthcoming Bromley stipulation, I said
I did not like the proposal made by Moore—that I myself
should seek a leave of absence from *Fortune*. In view of the
Time Inc./Brownell threat to my job, I thought I should require
Sloan to request my services from *Fortune* himself, in writing,

and that this letter should contain something that would serve as a protection from that threat. I said I could do that myself with Mr. Sloan when the time came, if it did.

On January 4, 1963, two days after Mr. Sloan's conference with Moore about a stipulation and his telephone exchange with me about it, Cravath sent my lawyers a draft of General Motors' stipulation. Instead of the simple one we had proposed on November 27, 1962, Cravath now proposed a more complicated one that included contingently my dismissal of the lawsuit, thereby starting an intense and seemingly rather hazardous legal contest in which the lawsuit could be won or lost depending on the way the stipulation was written.

Cravath for General Motors (January 4, 1963; received January 7) stipulated as follows:

SUPREME COURT: NEW YORK COUNTY

---

JOHN McDONALD, Plaintiff
        against
GENERAL MOTORS CORPORATION, Defendant

---

IT IS HEREBY STIPULATED AND AGREED:

1. That the activities, conferences and discussions among or between plaintiff, defendant, Alfred P. Sloan, Jr. and their respective counsel subsequent to the date upon which the summons herein was served upon defendant (March 2, 1962) shall be without prejudice to any and all rights and contentions herein of plaintiff and defendant, and shall not be made the subject of or constitute evidence, or otherwise be referred to, upon trial or in any other manner in this action, or in any other action or proceeding in which plaintiff, defendant, or Alfred P. Sloan, Jr. is a party;

2. That General Motors Corporation will not interpose any objection to the publication of a book (1) that is based upon the history of General Motors Corporation and the activities of Alfred P. Sloan, Jr. in connection therewith, (2) that is satisfactory to Alfred P. Sloan, Jr. and (3) that Mr. Sloan determines should be published, except that

it is further stipulated and agreed that Mr. Sloan, in reaching a decision with respect to the form, content or whether or not to publish such a book, may consult with anyone, including General Motors Corporation;

3. That in the event a book is published (1) that is based upon the history of General Motors Corporation and the activities of Alfred P. Sloan, Jr. in connection therewith and (2) that is satisfactory to Alfred P. Sloan, Jr. this action shall be dismissed with prejudice; and

4. That the time of defendant General Motors Corporation within which to answer or move with respect to the complaint herein is extended until 30 days following service upon attorneys for defendant of a written demand therefor by plaintiff.

January 4, 1963

Ennis objected to General Motors' stipulation mainly on two counts: that it was too broad, and that it put Mr. Sloan in the position of publishing to get General Motors out of a lawsuit. He discussed this with Barnum by telephone, and with me at length by telephone and letter, during the next several days. I then again took the shortcut and went in to see Mr. Sloan on January 18. It was a bit odd that we had no trouble meeting to discuss the conditions under which we should meet. I again wrote out on cards what I had to say to him, about the contest over the stipulation:

Since we met last October I have been eager to get together with you and see if we could work out something that everyone would be reasonably satisfied with. After we try it, I have assumed either we would have a book or we would know where we stood, and from there on reasonable men might know how to proceed.

I completed the American Smelting story for *Fortune* and on November 27th I offered Cravath-GM a stipulation to the effect that you and I should go to work on the book for a few months without prejudice to my position or theirs. After several weeks they objected that this would leave them in the situation where if you published a book to their liking but not to mine, I would still retain my legal position. They said that they wanted me to agree to withdraw my action if any book was published, even if I was unwilling to give my name to it.

During this time I reviewed in a general way, with Catharine, their revision of our book and came to you and gave you my opinion, in some detail, that it is not a valid book and not properly publishable by a man of your reputation and indeed by anyone. Our book, as you know, is valid, not only in your opinion but in the opinion of historians and publishers who studied it; and the facts in it were checked and approved in 1959 by GM's New York staff.

Although GM's recent revisions are not valid, I reported to you that I had not given up hope. The hope I had in mind was that some things that might be worrying them most might not be essential from our point of view and vice versa. We had to find that out by working together on specific points. But the problem then became one of setting the conditions under which we could work. As I have said, I proposed a simple stipulation setting aside all other matters while we made the try.

At the end of December I came to you again and reported my understanding of what was holding things up. You then stirred them up and on January 7, Cravath-GM sent my counsel a different stipulation.

The first paragraph of this stipulation was similar in principle to mine of six weeks earlier in proposing that "activities, conferences and discussions" be without prejudice to either party. They added, however, several new requirements as follows:

2. That General Motors Corporation will not interpose any objection to the publication of a book (1) that is based upon the history of General Motors Corporation and the activities of Alfred P. Sloan, Jr. in connection therewith, (2) that is satisfactory to Alfred P. Sloan, Jr. and (3) that Mr. Sloan determines should be published, except that it is further stipulated and agreed that Mr. Sloan, in reaching a decision with respect to the form, content or whether or not to publish such a book, may consult with anyone, including General Motors Corporation;

3. That in the event a book is published (1) that is based upon the history of General Motors Corporation and the activities of Alfred P. Sloan, Jr. in connection therewith and (2) that is satisfactory to Alfred P. Sloan, Jr. this action shall be dismissed with prejudice. . . .

There are several troubles with these paragraphs in their stipulation. They speak of "a book," not our book. Could they have in mind the invalid revision? Furthermore, they do not specifically mention our working together or give a time limit for that work. The numbered points in paragraph (2), while seeming to say something new, actually say what is and always has been the case.

You do not need a stipulation from me to publish a book with or without their approval and mine; nor do you need a stipulation from me to consult with anyone you please. We consulted with GM almost daily for five years. It makes a difference, however, if I agree to such words in a stipulation: it *seems* to shift the burden of responsibility from them to you, and you become responsible for the existence of the case. I do not want to put that pressure on you or bring you into this thing. I have taken care to keep you out of it. Furthermore, my counsel tells me that if I agree to such words, I jeopardize my case, and at the very least cause unnecessary confusion. If I were to do that, there is not likely to be any book. I have brought the book back to life and I can only keep it alive by maintaining my position.

As to paragraph (3): It describes the possible publication of a book which might be any book, or any conceivable revision of our book. It says that if such a book is published I should retire.

I do not believe that you would want to publish a book which did not meet the standards of historical scholarship and writing, which by profession I represent—it would not be to your interests, or anyone's, to do so. The integrity of your reputation and mine for all future time, as regards this book, depends upon the standards of our performance. May I observe to you that if I were only interested in economic gain and the least expenditure of effort, I would need only to accept their proposition and, you willing, publish GM's present revision of our book.

We are losing critical time while this fencing is going on. I'm proposing to them now a simple stipulation along the following lines:

1. That you and I go to work on the book to see if we can find a basis for publication and that this be done without prejudice to my position or theirs.

2. That if a book is published that is agreeable to you and me, I withdraw my action.

3. That we take three months to reach a conclusion and, if it is favorable, arrange to have the book published within nine months afterward. (I say nine instead of six months because after another three-month interval we will probably be too late to publish next fall, but could easily have it out by next January. It is unfortunate that the loss of time is making it impossible to publish at the best time, i.e., next fall.)

If this is not acceptable to them, I think we shall have exhausted effort along these lines, and we shall have to try some other way. Maybe you can think of something. We both want to see the book published. It is your life and seems to be consuming mine.

Mr. Sloan read my cards out loud, repeating certain sentences two or three times, and afterward returned to various passages several times.

He expressed himself as irked at Cravath's delay between my stipulation of November 27 and theirs of January 7. He repeated what he had said at earlier meetings, that he had been afraid their revisions would be invalid from the point of view of a sound book; that he did not know that they had revised our book until Tex Moore brought the revision to him; that a published book must have my name on it because his reputation was as involved in it as was mine; and that he depended on me to advise him on these matters. He laughed sympathetically when he read the last line to the effect that the book is his life and is consuming mine. There was a good deal of conversation back and forth and then he got down to the conflicting stipulations. He wanted to know if I had sent mine to Cravath. I said I had not but probably would on Monday; that meanwhile he and I had the opportunity to discuss it.

The sticking point, he observed, was point (2), namely that they allowed for a book without my name whereas I insisted that the book that was published must be agreeable to both him and me. He asked me point-blank if I would refuse a stipulation that permitted a book without my name. I said that as things are I would refuse it. He then said that he would go along with my stipulation, its three points, point (2) being the critical one. "I agree with it," he said. "I will call Mr. Moore in Monday morning and tell him."

He then asked whether I would come over Monday morning. "You don't mind seeing him [Moore], do you?" he asked. I said, "I don't mind seeing you. I don't know about him." Sloan laughed. He asked for the cards with the three points of my stipulation. I said these were my own cards, exploring it with him, and I would rather not leave them. He said, "I won't forget them."

On Monday, January 21, 1963, Mr. Sloan telephoned me via his new secretary, Miss Storch, who said, "Mr. Sloan wants me to give you this message, that he had an extended conference with Mr. Moore this morning and some ideas were developed which Mr. Moore will further develop without delay."

The next day, Tuesday, Barnum called Ennis and complained about my talking to Mr. Sloan. Ennis then called me, and related that Barnum was disappointed that I would not sign the Cravath-GM stipulation according to which I would withdraw the lawsuit if any book at all was published. Barnum had come to believe, in view of his previous discussion with Ennis, that I would sign the stipulation if GM would. Ennis replied that this was the result of a misunderstanding, and that he had in truth indicated only a willingness on my part to explore the GM line of thought. He said that he himself, after studying the stipulation, could not as my lawyer advise me to sign it. He reminded Barnum that we were unwilling to place the burden of the case on Mr. Sloan. Barnum had been of a different mind: "I had thought that we [my lawyers] would rely on John's influence over Mr. Sloan," he replied.

"So," Ennis said to me, "Barnum and Cravath are sore and disappointed." In addition, Barnum said that Moore was also "perturbed" because I upset Mr. Sloan as to what the difficulty has been. Barnum said that he doubted there would be a stipulation.

My lawyers were exasperated with the prolonged conflict over a stipulation, and the neglect of the main issues of the suit and the book. Bill Fitelson proposed an ultimatum. He recounted the events of the case, which had now run almost a year: how we had advised them of the action before beginning it, and afterward given them the courtesy of extensions, at their request, for them to investigate and consider it, with further extension to this time. During the time of the extensions, General Motors had "caused" (Fitelson's belief) the intervention of Time Inc., with its threat to my job if I did not discontinue the action. Without my knowledge or Mr. Sloan's, General Motors rewrote the book and proposed to have it published instead of the original, in lieu of any damages or reimbursement of legal fees. In Fitelson's opinion, General Motors was now trying to bring about a situation in which no book would be published. The passage of time, he thought, disregarding the Bradley proposal, worked against us in view of Mr. Sloan's age, as well as in our attempts to meet their proposals: We had gained nothing by waiting. Mr. Sloan wanted the book and had approved it. General Motors, after once approving it, had suppressed its publication. Fitelson proposed that in view of the way things were going, we should give General Motors until February 15 next to answer the complaint and proceed with the litigation. Our objective should continue to be a settlement, with General Motors buying out my proprietary interest and arranging to deposit the original book with Columbia University in order that it be made available to scholars after a period of ten years.

It was a strategy. A twenty-day ultimatum would get action of some kind. The situation for all parties was a pressure cooker, with my lawyers, fed up with the drag and stall, wanting action, Cravath's grip on Mr. Sloan loosened by the stipulation business, and General Motors in need of a new strategy on their side of the impasse.

In February Cravath sent another draft stipulation, which my lawyers immediately rejected. Barnum called Eddie about our rejection of it, and Eddie gave me a report of their conversation. It contained a radically new question.

Barnum had said that they were sorry our reaction came so promptly in writing, because they thought we would take more time. Eddie told him that we were currently exhausted on stipulations. Barnum asked whether we would consider some idea of the dimensions of the problem of the book: Was General Motors' version of the book so completely away that there was no use working on it? Eddie replied that I had said it was far off, and that he would pass on the question. Barnum then asked whether I should meet with Al Powers, the General Motors' chief counsel, instead of Mr. Sloan, to discuss the question of the dimensions of the problem with their revision. The outcome of such a conference could be finding that there was no common ground, or if common ground existed, a stipulation for three months' work, or uncertainty and no progress.

About my meeting General Motors' general counsel, Al Powers, the answer is no, presumably, said Eddie, beginning our talk about it a few days later. I said that a discussion of revisions would likely take a long time, as two out of three pages have some and they say there are more to come. Eddie said: There's been a big waste of time over the stipulation; I would like them to know how far apart we are on the book. It gives them a hard time. The lawyers disagree. There's room for disagreement. Eddie and I agreed that my position depended on a consensus of the lawyers on the stipulation and my desire to keep matters clear with Mr. Sloan. I said that I was not unwilling to show

General Motors my views on the book, but I needed to meet Mr. Sloan first in deference to him on procedure. We wanted a simple stipulation for a meeting with Al Powers; again there was the issue of a no-prejudice stipulation versus their still-evolving more complicated one with its provisions for my withdrawing the suit under certain conditions. Their view, said Eddie, is that the lawsuit is dead if *anything* is published; Bert, our hard-liner, will say "go to hell," take our stipulation word for word or no discussion, or else buy out my interest—leaving out the fact that both Mr. Sloan and I want the book, a fact that must remain clear. This was not the pleasantest climate for negotiating but it pressures them, Eddie observed, and they are saying to Mr. Sloan that they are trying; they will say that they asked for the meeting to learn the areas of difficulty. They will complain that my approval over what Mr. Sloan publishes gives me a veto. Eddie tells them no, it's just what the stipulation says. I've got a lawsuit. Eddie conjectured: if Mr. Sloan dies tonight, they buy me out and don't publish. Or, if he dies and has passed the decision on the book to others, they can say they will think about it for five years. They raised the question of General Motors publishing *their* work. We had to put a new point in our stipulation. For us, it's better to keep it simple.

Later that day Eddie called back to say he had talked to Barnum, and that Barnum had said the "Old Man" (Mr. Sloan) was pressing Tex Moore and Tex was on Barnum's head. He said he understood a stipulation would be given, of course. Presumably ours. The only thing dead, Barnum said, is that GM will not sign a stipulation that says McDonald has the decision on what book to publish. He said: What we are working toward is, what is the area of McDonald's reservations?

## March–April 1963

Despite uneasiness on both sides, we got a one-shot agreement and set March 20 as the date for meeting with Al Powers and others from General Motors—another "summit." The understanding was that Mr. Sloan would be there. On March 12, I went in to see him and bring him up to date, if he needed it, and to arrange to meet him and Catharine Stevens the day before the meeting with General Motors to go over a compromise that I would suggest we make. As usual, I gave him notes to read:

Since I last saw you I have continued to try to get an agreement on a stipulation under which we could work. Cravath-GM's stickiness on it has been obscure to me. However, something at least is happening, though it is not precisely what you and I have in mind. Cravath-GM has asked if I would meet with Al Powers to see how far apart we are on reaching an accord with the book, and presumably to determine whether they think it is worthwhile for you and me to work together over a period of time. Long ago I expressed my hope that we could reach an accord with GM and, as you know, suggested that you and I work for three months or so to that end, and if we reached agreement with GM, I would go on working as long as necessary to see the book through publication. But they wish to have this meeting to decide whether you and I should go ahead.

About this proposal, I replied that I would meet with Mr. Powers if you were also present. We have agreed on that and I have signed a stipulation for that meeting, and further meetings if that is the way it goes. I suggested a day next week. If this is agreeable to you, would Wednesday, the 20th—a week from tomorrow—be convenient for you? I expect that this question will be put to you soon by Cravath. I came over today to explain my part in it and to make a couple of suggestions.

I plan this weekend to study again in a general way their proposed revisions, and would like to meet with you, and perhaps Catharine (the three of us together), privately, and go over with you the compromises I think we can make without destroying the validity of the book. Of course, these will have to be generalized and simplified, as the proposed meeting will be a shorthand way of doing what you and I were going to do at length and in detail over a period of time. I suggest too that you might bring Catharine to the meeting to assist you and keep you posted on the parts of the book, etc., that will be under discussion. And would it be more convenient to have the meeting in the Foundation conference room where the sound can be amplified for you?

Mr. Sloan was agreeable to all this and arranged to meet with Catharine Stevens and me Tuesday, March 19, at 11 A.M. continuing through lunch (which he suggested we have together) and all day. He agreed to attend the Cravath-GM meeting on March 20 and would bring Catharine Stevens to assist him.

Two days later, however, I heard that Mr. Sloan would not be at the meeting on March 20. I sent him a message through Catharine Stevens, who went in to see him. Her record of their meeting reads:

I took the following message from John to Mr. Sloan at 4 P.M. today: "Cravath-GM lawyers say that you are not going to be present on Wednesday. Is this so? If it is, I think it is important that you and Catharine and I meet as planned on Tuesday. John"
Mr. Sloan took the note, and said, "That's right." He picked up a sheet of paper on his desk, which had four or so typewritten paragraphs on it, and held it in his hand with the note from John in front of it, but so that he could read from the large sheet of paper.
Mr. Sloan said: "Cravath, Swaine and Moore say that the meeting is to be an initial investigation, a study to learn what you want to do to the book, to get your position, in other words, in respect to the changes General Motors has suggested. For that reason they feel it would be unwise for me to be present."
Then Mr. Sloan looked at John's note again, and in reference to the last statement of it, said:
"Furthermore than that, they feel that we should not meet together on Tuesday as planned for the same reason. In other words, to repeat, what they want to do on Wednesday is to learn what you want to do to the book, to determine whether . . ." Mr. Sloan stopped looking at the sheet he had in his hand and said, "No, that's all right, stop there."
As I started to leave, he said, "Tell John I think it's all right."
I said, "All right for John to meet with them on Wednesday?"

He said: "Yes, I think it's all right. It's probably better for me not to be there."

These maneuvers indicated a major change in the position of General Motors. Unable to get anywhere with Mr. Sloan with their revision or the legalisms of stipulation for extended meetings between Mr. Sloan and me, they were now bypassing him and the impasse over that stipulation for our meeting for direct confrontation with me not about the suit—Cravath's obsession—but about the book itself—a sort of *editorial* meeting. In the absence of Ennis, who was away, I wrote a letter to Bert Mayers describing what I saw going on and raising some questions about it:

In view of the events today, I am concerned about certain aspects of the proposed meeting with GM-Cravath next Wednesday, March 20, and I want to pass these concerns on to you for your consideration.

First, I understood that I signed a stipulation last Tuesday to facilitate first of all a meeting with Al Powers of GM, Barnum of Cravath, Alfred Sloan, yourself and myself. If that was the understanding, then they have pulled a switch by directing Sloan not to appear at the meeting. Their motive, I understand, was to expedite the meeting which, they said, might be slowed down by Sloan's difficulty in hearing. I understand they also said that Sloan requested that he should be eliminated from the meeting; and that they said that Catharine Stevens would be at the meeting.

Now, I was somewhat persuaded by this line of thought, i.e., making fast progress at the meeting. But I was persuaded only because Sloan and I and Catharine Stevens had arranged to meet the day before, March 19, all day, starting at 11 A.M., through lunch at the RCA lunch club, and on through the afternoon, as long as it would take for us to agree on what revisions we would yield to GM to reach an accord on publication. On Tuesday last, March 12, I saw Sloan and explained the whole matter to him (see enclosed notes on that meeting). He said he agreed with what I said, and he immediately cleared his schedule to give the whole day, Tuesday and Wednesday next, to the two meetings.

Today Sloan made it clear that he had nothing to do with requesting that he stay out of the Wednesday meeting with Cravath-GM: he had, on the contrary, been ordered to stay out of it.

He made it clear to Catharine Stevens that it was he who did request that she go to the meeting and that Tex Moore was opposed to her being there and that this matter was still to be settled on Friday, March 15. Today he was still hoping that his request would be met.

Furthermore, and this is a real novelty, Cravath-GM forbid Sloan to meet with me next Tuesday. What has this got to do with expediting the meeting with Cravath-GM on Wednesday? Several implications of this move are running through my head but I can't pull them all out right now. One thing is clear, however, namely, that they are getting their way on their original request for me to meet with Powers, and with no one else. Another is that they are taking control of Sloan and my relations with him (this may not stick in the future—but they are exhibiting their power over him at the moment: this means, I think, that Sloan's role of decision is going to be limited to his refusal to publish a revised book without my approval: everything else is to be between GM and me, as they seem to see it).

I don't think Sloan is happy about this. He is still wanting to get in the middle and swing a valid book while they are maneuvering him out of the picture. But he is pretty old to buck the powers that be in this world. And although he is concerned about my reaction, he goes along on their directives. For Cravath-GM he is a problem, perhaps *the* problem. On balance, he cannot be counted on to do very much, but he is in a sort of way, in his posture, a powerful silent ally, and for better or worse will always be in the picture somewhere. For the moment, however, he is out of it except as they will have him in mind, and we are confronted purely with GM. That's the way it is, so OK.

I want to raise a couple of questions.

Have their actions with respect to the March 20 meeting been consistent with understandings reached in your talks with Barnum? If as it seems to me, they are not, what light does this cast on their good faith in requesting the meeting? Does it make any difference?

Is it proper for me to meet with the General Counsel of General Motors, rather than say Donner? In other words, does Sloan's absence and the block against my seeing him before the meeting change the character of the meeting? So far as my meeting only with their lawyers is concerned, perhaps it is the case that only Al Powers in GM knows the contents of the book and GM's objections well enough to discuss them with me. I don't know. I just raise the question. Except for Sloan, I never meet anyone but lawyers.

    In Sloan's message to me today via Catharine Stevens, he read from the Cravath instructions to him (see enclosed) a formulation of theirs that goes back to the day they presented their revision and that strikes me as dangerous. Sloan said something to the effect that the meeting was to be an initial investigation, a study to learn what I want to do to the book, to get my position in respect to the changes GM has suggested. Their formulation makes it seem that I am the one who is objecting to a book, i.e., their book; as if they were willing to publish a book but for my objections. I know you are perfectly aware of their tricks, but I want to call your attention to this one. Of course, I intend to talk about our book and the revisions I am willing to yield. But could there be a profound trick in calling this meeting to discuss, by their formulation, the book as revised by them? In a nutshell, are they misrepresenting the purpose of this meeting? Does it matter? . . .

    On March 15, Mr. Sloan telephoned me that he was canceling the meeting we had arranged on the 19th between him and Catharine and me, the all-day meeting where we were to review and discuss a compromise on the text of our book in preparation for the meeting on the 20th. That made it definitive: With Mr. Sloan out of even the preliminaries, on an assist from Moore, General Motors had got it down to a two-parties game—between them and me.

    Later that day I had a message from Catharine Stevens that she would be at the Wednesday meeting. That was an improvement.

    Still later that day I talked to Bert. He said that he wanted the meeting to go ahead as scheduled, and that he was waiting for a call from Barnum. My notes:

Telephone from Bert: He told Barnum I was disturbed. That I didn't understand the implications of keeping me from Sloan on Tuesday. That it was a return to the old atmosphere of coercion and suppression, that it was destructive.
Barnum: GM wants to know John's [illegible] narrow down. Hence the meeting. Discuss Sloan with Tex Moore.

Bert: Nothing doing. I will not talk to Tex Moore, but only to Cravath-GM.

Barnum: I will see what I can do.

On Monday they agreed on a stipulation for the March 20 meeting.

Matters between the lawyers having become tighter than ever, the meeting was likely to be a turning point to some new course. As throughout, I didn't want a court to decide the issues, any more than I presumed they did, though for different reasons. Nor did I want to separate the damage from the book and settle for damage without the book; nor I guessed did they, for while money damages for them would be only an item in the cost of doing business, the book would be a hot potato in their hands with Mr. Sloan refusing in my absence to publish their version of it. At a meeting of the lawyers, Mayers had sounded out Bromley on the question of settlement of the damages, the news of which traveled overnight to Mr. Sloan and caused him to protest to me through Catharine: "John can't have the book and the money too." Meaning, as I took it, that he would be dismayed if I gave up on the book. I don't know that the situation was in fact all that binary—book or money—but I am sure he spoke from knowledge as well as interest. I reassured him in a way that put some heat on him: "If I can't have the book, I want the money."

The odd question coming to the table on March 20 was whether I could, tolerably from my standpoint, yield what they wanted yielded without knowing what it was they wanted—and would never tell. The absence of particulars made me wonder whether they knew much about GM in the 1920s other than what they had read in the book. And further, their revision had so much failed my requirements that I did not care even to address it except for some negative observations in general.

The meeting, however, gave me an opportunity to direct a solution if I could find it: To deal with these complexities, I needed a concept, even if it failed to hit the nail on the head, something to work with that made real sense.

In the background from my standpoint, and in the foreground from theirs, was the government's antitrust investigation, which featured Bromley leading the General Motors defense. Although this had a bearing on their attitude toward the book, vaguely stated, as noted earlier, by Hogan and Bromley to Mr. Sloan and by him to me, I was not privy to anything more. I knew a little about it from newspapers after the Department of Justice had called the grand jury in early 1959. That grand jury, in a "broad probe" aimed at "undue concentration" in the automobile industry, had subpoenaed General Motors' documents back to 1929. This gave Cravath plenty of work to do, as the investigation was extended also to General Motors' nonautomotive divisions, where it led to an indictment of the locomotive division in April of 1961 on charges of monopoly. Legal skirmishing over the disclosure of documents in the automotive field led to contempt proceedings in November 1962. I have since learned that a dozen federal prosecutors worked over General Motors, with appearances by them or Cravath or both before ten Federal District Court judges in New York in the years 1959 through 1963.

But these affairs were theirs, to which my refrain was: What did these problems have to do with the book? My job was to defend the book, not General Motors. Still, as I prepared to meet representatives of General Motors on March 20, 1963, I speculated on what the opponents of the book might have against it. The stated issue was to be the distance between our original book and their revision. The thousands of words of changes tracked by Catharine across twenty-four chapters of our close-knit, well-researched, and well-checked manuscript made no sense on the face of it. It would, of course, have been bad strategy for them to have specified targets for the antitrust prosecutors. Logically, then, their myriad changes had served the purpose of radically altering the book without revealing which of the changes really mattered to them. The revised book thus kept their now four-year-old secret by means of a random strategy that in effect gave equal value to each of the changes, while leaving me with the problem of how to deal with ten thousand decoys. Perhaps they didn't know quite what they were afraid of, or they were afraid of everything, or of only a few things or areas in varying intensity across a range of possible antitrust actions. Perhaps they had thought that they could run their book past Mr. Sloan and me (for my royalties) and be done with it. That hadn't worked, and so now they wanted to meet again and talk about it.

In the brief time before the meeting, I went back through the project for a clue to General Motors' fear of the book. I read the record of the long discussion I had had on August 4, 1958 with Henry Hogan, the then General Motors' chief counsel who, not long after, would order the suppression of the book. Why he had waited until the last minute before publication to suppress might have had the trivial explanation that he hadn't got around to reading it until then: Hogan and Cravath probably learned more about the inside of the General Motors of the 1920s from the book than they had ever known before. It was a strange coincidence that the grand jury subpoenaed General Motors documents in the same month in 1959 as our meeting with Doubleday and agreement to publish; and even stranger that we started the book at about the same time—1954—that Herbert Brownell as Attorney General initiated the investigation of General Motors. The appearance of the grand jury subpoena was a pretty obvious factor in the suppression, but not by itself. There should be something real or imagined in the book that they were afraid of. Bromley's explanation to Mr. Sloan for suppressing the book—generalities and public information such as General Motors' share of the automobile market—was a dodge, or at any rate lacked substance as regards the book.

Reading over the record of my discussion with Hogan shortly before he suppressed the book, I looked for anything that might have anticipated his later drastic action and so reveal his specific motive. Hogan had been eloquent in opposing the very notion of "archives," as I recounted earlier, pinning Du Pont's loss of the government suit and their ousting from General Motors on their being an archive company, which, he said, General Motors was not. The particular item in the Du Pont archive that caused the suit, he had argued, was Point Five of the several reasons given in 1917 by John J. Raskob for expanding Du Pont's investment in General Motors, which refers to securing General Motor's paint purchases. Du Pont made the investment and further expanded it in the takeover from Durant in 1920, and eventually got a lot of the General Motors paint business for the Du Pont company. What interested me now was not the argument over what lost the suit for the Du Ponts and won it for the government, but Hogan's judgment that Raskob's Point Five had nothing to do with the outcome of the suit—and everything to do with starting it. It was only one sentence but, according to Hogan, it had been enough for the antitrust prosecutors to take to the Attorney General and get the okay to commence the suit.

The question was, for me, had Hogan found a line or a sentence in our book that he imagined an antitrust prosecutor could likewise take to an Attorney General to trigger an antitrust suit against General Motors? Would he kill the whole book for one line? The record of my talk with Hogan in August of 1958 offered no clue to any such particular line in the book, not surprisingly, as we had not talked about the book proper but only about a footnote on the Du Pont case, and Hogan, at the time, far from suppressing, was cooperating with us, then perhaps unaware that ours was an "archive" book.

That awareness would come and now in March of 1963, trying to understand the Hogan of 1958 and 1959, I took the following tack in thought. I wondered whether Hogan might be similarly applying his trigger theory of the Du Pont case to his own company, General Motors. I wondered, if there was nothing of substance in the book for them to worry about, could they be perceiving our book as a trigger, in much the same way that Point Five was in the Du Pont case? The kind of document an antitrust lawyer in the justice department could take to the attorney general to justify starting a suit? I was not aware of any revelations in the book that could convict General Motors of breaking an antitrust law. What I needed, then, in this study of the suppression, was a trigger line in our book equivalent to Raskob's Point Five. And I had such a line unknowingly since my conversation at lunch with Hugh Cox in Washington in the winter of 1961. Remembering it in this context was an eye-opener.

I had been so impressed with Cox's opinion, on his reading the book in manuscript, that it contained nothing to worry General Motors, that I had until this moment given little attention to the hedge he had taken. Cox was learned and experienced in the subject of antitrust law in general and General Motors in particular; there was really no better authority. It was as if the distinguished Acheson law firm of Washington, of which he was a star member, were dismissing the opinion of the distinguished Cravath law firm of New York that the book would destroy General Motors. But then there was the little exception he had taken that now came back to me with force: "except," he said, "maybe the line, 'A monopoly is not planned.'"

The sentence "A monopoly is not planned" occurs in the Product Policy of 1921—entitled "Future Manufacturing Lines of General Motors Corporation"—which was, as I have discussed earlier, the master plan for the new General Motors after the Du Pont takeover. Mr. Sloan and I had dedicated a chapter (chapter 4) of our book to that Product Policy and we had planned to put the original document in our appendix. As I have noted, the policy features a market strategy of "covering the market for *all* grades of automobiles that can be produced and sold in large quantities," sloganed as "a car for every purse and purpose." Presented in overlapping price classes, the expected volume for each gave the whole a more or less pyramid shape, Chevrolet across the wide bottom, Cadillac at the narrow top. The policy's uniqueness at the time lay in its proposed dynamic interactions with the competition across each price class. It was aimed then particularly and by name at Ford who had only two grades, with the Model T at the bottom and the Lincoln at the top. Afraid to compete head-on with the Model T, which "practically monopolized" the first grade, GM put this interactive pyramid strategy to work on the Model T below and the others above the Chevrolet.

From this concept had also come a new car, the Pontiac, which was designed as a closed car with production economies overlapping Chevrolet and brought out strategically in 1926 to fill the gap in price class between Chevrolet and Olds, thereby to protect the top of the Chevrolet market from the same kind of invasion that Chevrolet was making into the top of Ford's market. With the Oakland soon phased out, the GM phalanx and its economies of scale settled at the ongoing sets of five car lines: Chevrolet, Pontiac, Olds, Buick, and Cadillac.

This was the strategy that won the market, outplaying Ford in the 1920s, and that eventually, out of competitive necessity, was adopted by Ford and Chrysler, who with GM became the "Big Three." In the long run, especially in the Depression 1930s, they survived while most other automobile companies— ones with only one or two price classes—dropped out. It didn't create a classic monopoly, but it led to the economists' neoclassical "oligopoly" of General Motors, Ford, and Chrysler, together representing 90 percent of the U.S. market, stable for many years until penetrated by competition from abroad.[2]

Coexisting with this strategy in the General Motors Product Policy of 1921 was the technological strategy, aimed to win fast and big with Kettering's copper-cooled engine. In the midst of specific plans for the changeover from water-cooled to air-cooled engines, they wrote another abjuration of monopoly: "It should not be the desire of the corporation to monopolize the motor car field. . . ." This also referred to covering the market in price classes, but, in context, mainly with the copper-cooled engine.

Had the new engine lived up to Kettering's and Pierre Du Pont's revolutionary expectations, General Motors would very

---

2. "Oligopoly" is an economists' word for a defined market with a small number of sellers, each of whom has some influence over price, different from the classical model of a competitive market with many participants, none of whom individually can influence price. The interactive models of game theory shed some light on the strategic, interactive character of General Motors' Product Policy, which was designed in advance of its application like a theoretical model. As the policy was designed and recorded by the automotive group in General Motors headed by Mr. Sloan, and as he participated in our account of it in the book, it seems fair enough to call it his strategy.

likely have had a monopoly, and so a monopoly problem in the technology, for a time anyway. As it was, General Motors was lucky to survive the failure of the engine—lucky, that is, to have had Mr. Sloan around to keep the water-cooled engines ready for the boom market of 1923.

There were other worthy one-liners and sentences in the Product Policy, one of considerable cultural as well as business interest: "The primary object of the General Motors Corporation . . . is to make *money,* not just to make motor cars" (their emphasis). This declaration of purpose may have been a general one of an ethos or culture and discipline of business, or it may have been aimed, rather like the Chevrolet itself, at Henry Ford's business philosophy. Ford had had complaints from John and Horace Dodge and other early Ford investors, that he was obsessed with cars and more cars, not profits. The Dodges actually sued Ford, accusing him of being interested not in making money, but only motorcars—more and more Model Ts. They won the suit, and Ford bought out the Dodge interest in his company, giving him total control of the Ford Company. Ford said, "If you give them all that [high wages, low prices], the money will fall into your hands: you can't get out of it." This philosophy served Ford well for seventeen years, from 1908 to 1925. After this his obsession with the out-of-date Model T, and the absence of any other product policy to counter Mr. Sloan's strategy as represented in the GM Product Policy statement of 1921, resulted in his having to take a back seat to General Motors.

Putting money before cars would also one day open the door for a "Ralph Nader" interpretation of the policy and practice of the company. The money concept in any case was a bold statement of both the culture and the discipline of the business, which Mr. Sloan subscribed to again in the book, although he associated money with operations and had a distaste for detached speculation.

The authors of the General Motors Product Policy, it appears, were worried about the consequences of success and wanted to declare in advance that if it happened to result in a monopoly, it had not been their intention. I don't know if their stated worries of 1921, when Hogan later read them in our book, brushed off on him in 1959 and caused him to ban the book—the lawyer as enemy of history. Studying the matter before the meeting set for March 20, 1963, in the absence of actual knowledge of the cause of the ban, I adopted the hypothesis that something like that had happened, Hogan's trigger being the same as Cox's exception to General Motors' innocence.

It had become clear that Mr. Sloan would accept any solution I proposed, if I could get it past General Motors. Now, with the essential game down to two sides, mine and General Motors', and as a court decision threatened undesirable results for either or both sides, I decided to offer a settlement I thought might get around their lawyers' objections while still satisfying essential criteria for a valid book. Their stated objection to the book—General Motors' size and market share—being information in the public domain, hence irrelevant to the book, I could put enough heat on them, I thought, to force them to sort out their secrets and test them against my proposed compromise, with the alternative that we go to court. The essential value for me was to publish a valid book at that time. I had no definite idea of how to deal in the future with the confirming documents, particularly the Product Policy.

On the basis of this concept I wrote a statement, which I proposed to read at the meeting, outlining a compromise that I thought Mr. Sloan and I could make without losing the validity of the book.

Catharine Stevens met Mr. Sloan the day before the March 20 meeting. She gave me a record of their meeting:

To Mr. Sloan, Catharine commented, "Too bad you can't be there."
Mr. Sloan replied, "I feel that way, too. I feel it proper to make these suggestions to John [all about compromises]. John can't be arbitrary any more than I can. Otherwise we won't get any book. I am not in the conference, so they can't quote me on anything. Maybe the meeting will come out with something that is not as good as what we have. Pretty good, but not as good as I would like to see it. This is a preliminary meeting. Anything Barnum and Brooks say is not necessarily final."

She brought up the subject of executives reviewing it, Bradley, Donner, and others. Mr. Sloan said, "Legal Department didn't see it." "See what?" (He meant the reply.) She asked him, "You understand [the] revisions?" "No." Catharine noted that he wanted to be impartial.

I read her record of their meeting at the time as saying to me not to quit if things didn't go well at the meeting; Mr. Sloan is cautiously hopeful of a willingness on GM's side to come away from their revision; he advises me not to be arbitrary, a statement by which he would mean that I should give them my reasons for the position I am taking, and that I should try to understand theirs. We might lose some things and still have a pretty good book.

As I didn't see Mr. Sloan on the 19th, I didn't give him a copy of the proposal I intended to make at the meeting.

I came early to the meeting on the 20th, with the proposal, which I had just finished writing that morning. Catharine came to the meeting and made a record for Mr. Sloan and ourselves, which is summarized below. Al Powers did not show. George Brooks came from Donner's office. I could see from the absence of La Rowe, author of the revisions, as well as of Powers, who had initiated the meeting, that there was probably no one present to defend their revisions editorially. Present at the meeting were Mr. Barnum, of Cravath, Swaine, and Moore; George A. Brooks, secretary of the General Motors Corporation; myself; Mr. Mayers; and Miss Stevens. Catharine Stevens's notes observe: "Mr. McDonald was making notes on some papers as the parties gathered. When he finished, he said that he would like to read a statement if it was all right with them. It was." I began to address the group:

I have come here to try to achieve the publication of Mr. Alfred P. Sloan Jr.'s and my book, "The General Motors Story," and to do so on the basis of maintaining the validity it possesses now in its original form. For this purpose I am prepared to discuss your alterations of our book, and to yield to a number of them where they do not affect the validity of the book. When I have concluded the statement I am reading on the subject, I want to make a comment on the arrangements for this meeting.

First, allow me to make an observation on the scale of the problem of discussing your alterations. You have made changes on 536 of the book's 783 pages, that is, on nearly seven pages out of ten. These break down into changes on 241 out of 371 pages in volume I, and on 295 out of 412 pages in volume II. These quantities, together with their qualitative aspects—the changes in the substance of the book—convert the book into a different kind of product, and raise obvious difficulties in simplifying the discussion.

There is something strange in the quantity of these alterations in view of the fact that they come up on top of the accommodations we made to General Motors during the preparation of the book. As you know, consultations were held with General Motors constantly by Mr. Sloan and myself during the years it took to do the book. In the course of this work, the chapters were reviewed by the ranking executives of the Corporation in each branch of its operations, and were reviewed by and at all times available to the top line, staff, and policy executives. The entire, completed book, furthermore, was checked out as to its facts by General Motors. . . . I should observe right here that these are not constructive changes. They confuse both the logic and the history of General Motors' financial control. . . .

All together, the large quantity and mixed character of the alterations has the effect of obscuring the location of your serious objections to our book. . . . Despite these difficulties in your concept of the book and in the manner and substance of your alterations, I shall, as I have said, make a practical effort here to accommodate you within the framework of a valid book, in order to lift its suppression and get it published. Let me put it to you broadly. I shall yield to you substantially all of your alterations in volume II. I am able to do this because volume II has had the peculiar character of being in the nature of a supplement to volume I. Its chapters are discrete, that is, separate and without continuity, each being marked by its specialized subject matter. It is like a bonus for those readers who have an extended interest in the subject matters, such as distribution, overseas, etc. As we are not obligated to extend these discussions, I shall repair the volume, where necessary, by re-working it and we will have a valid volume. I shall have some work to do here but no conceptual problem. Furthermore, I will strike out entirely the last chapter (twenty-four), "Why the Whole of General Motors Is Greater than the Sum of Its Parts," in which you seem, from the alterations made to it, to have a great deal of negative interest, and which does not represent a conceptual problem for me: I doubt that I could repair the damage done to it. . . .

Now as to volume I, we have an entirely different situation. This volume deals with General Motors' past both chronologically and logically, and the two aspects are rigorously related to form the structure and movement of the book. The chronology falls into six main periods: 1908–1920, 1920–29, 1936–41, 1941–45, and 1945–59. The logic stems from the development of three major General Motors policies, relating respectively to (1) product, (2) finance, and (3) organization. . . .

The major policies which operated critically to bring about these events between 1920 and 1929, were conscious intellectual activities in the leadership of General Motors, probably the most remarkable in American industrial history. They not only brought the General Motors Corporation to leadership and to the no. 1 position among all corporations in the United States, but they laid down conceptually a sound basis for the workability and development of the large corporation as a type of economic institution; in fact, these policies established the dominant pattern of large industrial operations in the United States. These, (1) the Product Policy, (2) the financial policy, and (3) the organization policy, unified into the logical foundation of General Motors, and arising from the ideas and activities of Mr. Sloan, the

Du Ponts, and others in the leadership of General Motors, are also the foundation of the book. . . .

Now again, to avoid suppression of the book, I am willing to make concessions in volume I. . . . In addition to [these] concession[s], I am willing to make another that I imagine will be of interest to you. In the interests of ending the suppression I am prepared also to yield the appendix, in which a number of documents appear verbatim. For Mr. Sloan and me this is a massive concession. . . .

Catharine Stevens then wrote: ". . . McD [then] reviewed what he was yielding in volume I: The quotation marks on the Product Policy, the appendix, and minor changes." I continued:

However, it appears from this that you recognize that in the absence of interference, Mr. Sloan and I will continue to see eye to eye, as we always have, on the necessity of maintaining a valid book. A man in his position, the dean of American businessmen, whose name in American history is known everywhere, and who is a great figure in the academic world, and in the philanthropic world as well as the business world, could not do otherwise, and I could not advise him otherwise, than to stand by the discipline of a valid book; for we are not dealing here with fiction but with the facts of American history, which are not revocable.

Having made this protest against keeping Mr. Sloan and me apart, I hope that sort of thing will stop and that we will get on a constructive basis, and move along with our concept of the book, as I think it is proper that you should. We can then proceed with the publishing contract, long since offered to us, and I shall work with Mr. Sloan for the time required to work out these changes and see the book through publication.

I made notes of Barnum's response: "I think you have made a very constructive statement with respect to [the] possible ways of working out the book. First, I will address myself to your comment at the end. . . . I don't resent your saying [continued] suppression, but I will deny that as the reason. We recognize that you and Mr. Sloan do see eye to eye on what would be a valid book. We understand you have met with Mr. Sloan to discuss the alterations, and Mr. Sloan says this is too much for me to grasp and I am relying on you to advise me. We have to live with that and can't [change it]."

The next day, March 21, I gave Mr. Sloan a copy of the proposal and summarized it for him, pointing out the two main concessions: that we would remove the quotation marks from the texts of the Product Policy of 1921 in chapter 4 and paraphrase the quoted material, and that we would cut the appendix of original documents. I observed to Mr. Sloan that this would reduce the quality of the book, depriving it of many confirming documents, but would keep its validity in the common way of a memoir. We would reject entirely and give no consideration to their revision of volume I but would let them have entirely their revision of volume II, and there would be some updating, where needed, from 1959 to 1963.

Mr. Sloan agreed with the compromise and so joined me in offering it to General Motors. After the next GM board meeting Mr. Sloan said to Al Powers: "If this doesn't work, we are at the end of the rope." Mr. Sloan said that he would not give Mr. Moore the summarizing page or the copy of my settlement proposal of yesterday but would let him make his own notes. I was glad to see him keep that distance between Moore and me. A few days later, he offered a contribution to our promised revision of chapter 4:

To: Miss Catharine Stevens
From: Alfred P. Sloan Jr.
Re: The General Motors Story
    Will you pass on the following note to John, if you please.
    With reference to your refashioning Chapter 4, I am inclined to think, although I have taken this entirely out of my mind, that what is to be avoided and eliminated, both factually and by implication so far as we can avoid it, is, any indication that the language might imply a determined purpose to monopolize the market.

I am rather inclined to think, although no one has told me so that the phrase "A Car For Every Purpose" might be construed to so imply. On the other hand of course it is perfectly absurd to think that an aggressive producer would evaluate the problem in any way differently and although at the time of this writing no producer so far as I recall was making more than one model, nevertheless the fact remains that a manufacturer making shoes, or retailer selling shoes, would not be so dumb as to think he could build a big shoe business by making one size shoes. He must make all sizes and all varieties to have a comprehensive business.

This is submitted as thinking it might help us.

[signed]

Alfred P. Sloan Jr.

Whether Mr. Sloan's worry about the language of monopoly in the Product Policy came straight from him or by way of General Motors' lawyers, it confirmed or at least paralleled my concept of this matter. It was my idea of combining Hogan's trigger theory with Cox's identification of the only line in Mr. Sloan's book that might be bothering GM—which had inspired my compromise offer, potentially giving breathing space to General Motors' lawyers in their homemade legal straitjacket. In any case Mr. Sloan had made the compromise and its concept his own. Whether as tactic or truth did not matter to me, since in my view, backed by Cox's authoritative reading, there was, in the book, nothing illegal to justify its suppression by GM. Mr. Sloan, however, was also raising the question whether the line "A car for every purse and purpose" might be attacked. By itself, as noted, it was a powerful and most successful concept. Combined with a putative intent to monopolize, it could presumably among lawyers create an arguable case for monopolistic conduct. But to make this case one would have to contend that the written denial of plan or desire to monopolize meant the opposite of what it says.

The language of monopoly appeared explicitly twice in the Product Policy in connection with General Motors, both times in the negative as "not planned," and "not to be the desire." It also occurred once in connection with Ford: "The field for cars of the first (lowest) grade is now practically monopolized by the Ford. At present it is being invaded by Chevrolet." Thus in the Product Policy, the language of monopoly appeared twice for General Motors in renunciation of any intent to monopolize, and once in attribution to Ford's domination of his low-price class.[3]

Sandy Parker, *Fortune*'s chief economist, and I moonlighted a study of chapter 4 and its subject, the Product Policy document, "Future Manufacturing Lines of General Motors Corporation." Sandy liked to take walks within the range of his apartment on Manhattan's East 53rd Street, and walking with him was always a personal and intellectual privilege. He had often discussed the book with me, and later the suit. So he was familiar with the subject. The problem was to paraphrase the quoted texts: Paraphrasing brought out the indeterminacy of translation, as indicated in these notes from our speculations about General Motors and their fear of a government suit:

---

3. Years later, using a game theory model of General Motors versus Ford in my book, *The Game of Business* (Doubleday, 1975), it came out that had Henry Ford played as rationally as Mr. Sloan, making the available countermoves to those in General Motors' Product Policy, he need not have lost his dominant position in the automobile market. Mr. Sloan's strategy, as described in the Product Policy of 1921, was not the inevitable winner. Ford, playing very poorly in the 1920s, holding on to the Model T beyond its time, handed it to him. Intuitively this was clear enough in the text of the book itself during the contest with General Motors over its suppression, but their lawyers had another way of imagining things, and that was my problem in getting the book out.

What might GM's lawyers be thinking would be the government's case? The government could say the Product Policy is muscle. Coordinated and planned to muscle others out. Was that their intention? That's subjective. Car sales by price classes might prove the attack was on Ford. They used the word "invading." How many cars are there in the first two price classes, including Ford, ninety percent? With Ford then having about fifty-five percent in units, Chevrolet four percent (and with the big future in that area).

The Product Policy is laden with circumstances, problems and policy. They had internal conflicts between staff and line, division and central office.

GM's own car lines are empty at the bottom of the price pyramid and crowded with six car lines in the middle; only Buick and Cadillac were making money. Sloan would have thrown all the others out, he said, before he would endanger Buick's profits.

As it was [under Durant] they had a collection of cars but no concept. They designed the product line to make money.

The significance, historically, is that you make better strides by reviewing what you are doing and what business is about.

Sounds funny in the modern world [1960s] but has the flavor of the times [1920s].

They think it over and say we are starting from scratch. Raises complexities. Intellectual fascination.

Merit is the extraordinary value for policy conclusions and planning to make processes of capitalism explicit.

They outline the chief purposes that presumably underlay any operation in any corporation, generalized, particularly standards of investment which no one in business to my [Sandy's] knowledge had written down. Here they wrote it for the first time to get their own people oriented. Quite rare: formulating initial principles.

Sloan had problems with two sets of people and the competition, that is, Kettering and Pierre vs. the Divisional people (with whom Sloan sided), and the low-price, big-volume market which Ford appeared to have a lock on. Possibly no one wanted to do anything about this problem, which could sink the U.S. Treasury if you tried to go against Ford head on. Except Kettering and Pierre, who had the idea of a revolutionary car. Sloan needed a blanket policy to cover all three problems. This can be stated objectively.

The circumstances existed.

The Product Policy did cover them.

The only thing we lack is documentary evidence of intention. Make clear: circumstance, problems, policy. Then the inference.

Against this background we got the quote marks out and the chapter paraphrased. This accomplished, I sent the new draft of chapter 4 to Mr. Sloan. At the end of March we met at his office with George Brooks, who found the chapter satisfactory. Shortly after, on April 2, I received this message from Catharine:

Mr. Sloan called me over to his office at 10:30 A.M. today. He had attended the General Motors Board Meeting yesterday at GM in NYC.

He said: Would you tell John that I have had a couple of minutes' talk with Al Powers at the General Motors meeting yesterday. I told Al that this was the end of the road, and I felt that if they couldn't approve this,* they couldn't approve anything, (You better call him Mr. Powers, Mr. Sloan said to me.) He indicated that the revision of chapter 4 was satisfactory so far as he was concerned. He said there were one or two minor points that he wanted to speak to Mr. Donner about but I got the impression that they were favorably disposed about it. This is no guarantee; this is only an impression. We have to wait the formal approval of Mr. Moore [*sic*].

Mr. Sloan also said: "If they approve, I want to sit down with you and John and work out a plan of operations."

*[Catharine added: Mr. Sloan meant chapter 4 revised, and approved by him March 29, and the other revisions proposed by Mr. McDonald in his statement to Mr. Brooks and Mr. Barnum.]

As I was suing General Motors and not Mr. Sloan, I presumed that he wanted Moore's "formal approval," with the emphasis on "formal." But Moore, in constant conflict of interest, either didn't understand the problems or was still working against the book.

On April 9, Mr. Sloan called Catharine over again and gave her the message for me, which he had received from Moore, saying Cravath was trying to get a new stipulation for proceeding to publication and was being frustrated by my lawyers. This persuaded Mr. Sloan to say, as he put it to Catharine: "What John wants is to publish and a suit to go on. [That's] illogical."

Not only was that illogical, but it was grossly mistaken. Moore had simplistically reflected and thereby misrepresented to Mr. Sloan a whole new round of lawyer issues over dates, contracts, revokes, actually agreeing to publish, preparations for publishing, actually publishing, legal expenses, and terminating the suit. Debate over these issues kept us from further direct action on the book until near the end of April, when Mr. Sloan and I began a series of meetings between us, with calls to lawyers, to try to resolve the issues ourselves.

Progress toward publishing came from my side, as it had from the beginning. Cravath was passive, resisting, delaying, and offered nothing constructive for the book. We made the constructive moves. The lawyers of that famous firm were presumably doing their best for their client, directing or being directed by General Motors' inside counsel, as they saw their interests, leaving Mr. Sloan's interest in the book out of consideration or to be considered only marginally. Mr. Sloan's lawyer Moore came into view only with replicas of the Cravath-GM positions, his place being taken over from time to time by Barnum of Cravath. A funny thing, that only I with my lawyers constructively represented the book—along with Mr. Sloan, of course, though he had no grip of his own on it. Then as I put the heat on him with a work deadline of mine at *Fortune*, which if missed could put everything off and into uncertainty again, Mr. Sloan put the heat on Cravath for a settlement. Cravath reacted in a slow, grudging retreat. Yet they seemed not to know how to play a cooperative game with someone who was not in their insiders' network. They seemed almost naïve in that respect, and that could hardly be. Something else must have kept them boxing.

At the third of these endgame meetings with Mr. Sloan, I presented him with eleven cards, which he read slowly. They contained the following:

I would like to conclude the whole matter now and go to work with you starting Wednesday [it was then Monday] to get the book out by Christmas.

Or, go to work with you now with a view to a publishing contract in ninety days, and publication at the earliest date the publisher can make on that basis.

The thing we need to know now is, what their [i.e., Cravath-GM's] objections are.

Can you find out?

Time is running out on us. In a few days I'll be into another *Fortune* story for a couple of months. If we don't get some constructive action this week, where does that leave us?

When he had finished reading, Mr. Sloan said that he wanted to call Barnum at Cravath. He asked whether he could keep the notes I had shown him until he had spoken with Barnum, and assured me that he would not give them or show them to Barnum but would return them to me. He had me tell his secretary, Miss Storch, to call Barnum.

Later that day I called Catharine to ask how Mr. Sloan had made out. She went to see him:

April 29, 1963, 4 P.M.

"Mr. Sloan, John called, and wondered if you'd had a chance to talk to Mr. Barnum."

Mr. Sloan replied, "I had a message from Mr. Moore. Tell John I have a message from Mr. Moore indicating that the legal fees are a limiting feature. He has been working on it and expects to get it cleared up tomorrow. That is his hope."

I told him that there are other factors which must be resolved here and have asked him to send Mr. Barnum up to me tomorrow so that I may get a better understanding of the facts contained in the note which you gave me and which I still have.

At 4:15 P.M. Miss Storch called and said, "Would you please tell Mr. McDonald that Mr. Sloan said Mr. Barnum will be here at 10:30 tomorrow morning."

## May 1–7, 1963

Mr. Sloan met Barnum, and the next day, May 1, Mr. Sloan and I met and talked over the things they had said. Immediately afterward I wrote an account of our meeting. Mr. Sloan announced that we would now have a publishing contract, a settlement of my expenses (legal fees) by GM, and an agreement between him and me starting that day, May 1, to work on getting the book out. According to Mr. Sloan, Barnum had told him that GM had offered to pay my (legal) expenses several days ago, and that they had not yet heard from my counsel. GM proposed to pay $25,000. Mr. Sloan stated that there should be no advance received from the publisher until the delivery of the manuscript, and that there could be no July date for delivery— even though the Matson-Doubleday contract, on his desk, called for a July 1 delivery. He said that he doubted we would complete the manuscript by that time, but might be able to do so by September.

Mr. Sloan also said that Mr. Moore would arrange my leave of absence from *Fortune,* and on a month-to-month basis instead of a six-month agreement; it would not be necessary, he said, for him (Mr. Sloan) to write to *Fortune.* Furthermore, Mr. Sloan proposed that Matson should distribute the royalties so that they did not come under his name.

We discussed each of these points.

I said that the publisher would ask for a delivery date. Mr. Sloan did not oppose it and I do not know what he did about it or what Barnum proposed to do.

I said the Doubleday advance should be paid now, when the contract is signed, as was customary. Sloan asked me if I wanted the advance now, and I said I thought it should be paid now, although I did not specify how I would like the payments made.

Mr. Sloan asked me to read the contract that Matson had sent over and voice my opinion. I said I would have my counsel study it just as his counsel and Barnum would study it.

I suggested he should write a letter to *Fortune* regarding my leave. He replied that he would have to speak to Mr. Moore about that.

I asked whether it was understood that we now had a book that was approved, and Mr. Sloan answered in the affirmative. I asked whether he was saying that he was planning to put a revoke into the contract. No, no, he answered. Is this going to be a binding contract? I asked. He said yes.

Actually, nothing was quite settled. But we had a new subject of discussion—my legal expenses. It was agreed that General Motors would pay them, as part of the settlement with the amount still open but bracketed between General Motors' offer of $25,000 and a proposal we had made of $50,000. Eddie had then proposed to split the difference, but Barnum had replied, with a quote from Donner, that their offer "was damn good pay, a reasonable offer, and [we] should regard it as adequate." That, coming from the C.E.O., seemed to have taken the matter out of Barnum's hands.

When I saw Mr. Sloan again on May 3, he had on his desk a note or letter from Barnum, which he showed me. It contained the information that my counsel wanted $37,500 for legal fees. Mr. Sloan told me that General Motors had refused. So, he said, we are held up.

I told him that Mr. Barnum's note about my legal expenses was not the real problem—that it was only a side thing and not worth talking about until we got the main issues settled.

Mr. Sloan said, "The money's important."

(He's telling *me* the money's important!)

He let it stand at that, from an inside track, leaving me to wonder why my, I thought modest, legal fees mattered so much: Was it to get Cravath's fees down? Mr. Sloan had once complained to me that they were high. Of course, given the formal hierarchy of General Motors' affairs, after Donner had made his judgmental ("damn good pay") counteroffer of $25,000—his first operational appearance in the lawsuit—there was no one around but Mr. Sloan with the standing to negotiate further, and Mr. Sloan would not want to give offense to Donner. There was also a question regarding which of them was the most uncomfortable—Mr. Sloan for the trouble his book had been giving General Motors, or Donner who, as chief executive, was officially responsible for having approved its suppression. There was another thing. Mr. Sloan himself refused to pay General Motors' bills; Donner had stated the maximum amount he was proposing to pay, and which he probably could take without specific recording, like petty cash. Any amount over that would have to come from somewhere else—like Mr. Sloan's personal bank account. So it would be tight between Donner and Sloan, although Sloan had undertaken the negotiation with me. I said that perhaps we could talk about splitting the difference between Donner's $25,000 and my lawyers' $37,500—I would have to talk to my lawyers about that. I said to him:

I would like General Motors to pay my expenses. I don't want to tell Barnum this—it's not wise—but if GM wants to force me to pay the extra $12,500 I'm not going to let that get in the way of our book. If I have to, I'll pay it. But I don't believe that can be a real issue, even for them. The real issues are: (1) consent to the manuscript; (2) a genuine contract with a delivery date; and (3) you and I get going next Monday on the routines of getting the book out.

Before we talked further about the legal expenses, Mr. Sloan said that he would speak to me about Mr. Barnum's letter.

With the change of subject, I handed him my cards on which I addressed him sharply on the subject at hand—the publishing contract. We stopped talking as he started reading:

Mr. Barnum told my counsel that the publishing contract they are preparing has in it an option to extend or withdraw—in other words, it is a revoke contract.

I thought we had GM's consent to the manuscript but this seems to imply that we do not. A revoke contract is no contract, it is not essentially more than an option to Doubleday.

That would appear to mean that we have made no progress—we are back where we started. Our problem here is to get GM's consent.

Mr. Sloan stopped reading here to say: "I want an irrevocable contract just the same as you do. I want you to be party to the contract. I depend on you. I've got to have you. What is holding us up is you being party to the contract. The only reason for 'discretion' was to get you party to contract."

"I thought we had a book," I said.

"So did I," Sloan responded.

I said, "I think the book is OK now."

He looked at Barnum's notes from the day before yesterday, and he showed me them. They read, "'discretion' in contract."

I said, "Discretion is revoke."

Mr. Sloan asked, "Will you take $31,000?" Barnum telephoned at this point and I went out while he talked to him. While out, I called Ennis to ask what he thought of another split to $31,000. He said OK. When I went back into Mr. Sloan's office, we resumed talking about legal expenses. I gave him a note in pencil, which he pocketed, reading, "$31,000 expense is okay.—John McDonald." He said, "Binding contract on delivery, July 1, with option to September 1." I would be party to the contract, and legal expenses would be $31,000. Mr. Sloan said, "Barnum is coming up here now. You go into another office." He took me into Bradley's office in the Foundation, and said that he would talk to Barnum and go back and forth between us. "I want to settle this this afternoon," he said.

After meeting with Barnum while I waited in Bradley's office, Mr. Sloan came back to me and explained that there were complications. Barnum said that $31,000 would be OK, and that he would arrange a stipulation on that with my counsel. But there was a question about a firm commitment. Mr. Sloan said that he was aware that I wanted a firm commitment, and he said: "I want a firm commitment, too. But, this is going to take some time." Money! Time! I said: "So let's you and I go to work on the manuscript [preparing it for publication]—that's what counts—and forget the rest."

Four days later, on May 7, Mr. Sloan balked. He called me over and showed me a letter he was sending to Barnum, in which he said that we could not do the job by September 1. He said that he did not understand why I was so anxious to get the book published. He said that he would try to sell a new program (Barnum's? Moore's?) to me containing no delivery date and a month-to-month contract with me for six months. He would be willing to advance me my share of the avoided Doubleday payment in order to satisfy my pressure to publish.

My publishing program may have looked formidable to his inexperienced eye, but that was not what was worrying him. On cards, I wrote:

Mr. Sloan, the details in my publishing program here do not prove that we do not have a manuscript now. I am willing to send it now, new chapter four, their revised volume II, GM's updating figures. I am ready. If Barnum wants to work along to get a manuscript satisfactory to him and us—that is the *only* question—I will work with you.

I asked him why, if he believed it would take us longer than a September 1 date, he wanted a contract with me that he could revoke month-to-month. While I committed to six months, he committed to only one. This revoke posture, a Cravath habit, meant to me that they were thinking not to publish but to go on blocking the book. Mr. Sloan asked me when the publisher had in mind to publish. I said that if they could have the manuscript by July 1, they would publish in January 1964, with books out before Christmas. That schedule favored my pressure to publish—it could be now or never.

Mr. Sloan then said that Moore would arrange my leave of absence from *Fortune* on a month-to-month basis. I demurred, reminding him that in a number of possible circumstances, including his own death, I might have to fight to get back to *Fortune*. It was thus better, from my standpoint, for him to write a letter including, as usual, that he expected I would return to the magazine. "Why is that a problem?" I asked. He responded that it was not a problem, but that he would have to speak to Moore first.

The letter was important. Creating an understanding between Mr. Sloan and Time Inc. that I expected to return to *Fortune* after working with him would disarm Time Inc. of its still-standing Brownell threat to my job. Should Time Inc. refuse that understanding, the consequences would have been potentially explosive—my position being that the loss of my job would be met with an instant lawsuit against Time Inc.—in the days when lawsuits were less common and not to be taken lightly. So it was no wonder that Moore tried to prevent Mr. Sloan from writing the letter that was in effect blocking any further action by Time Inc. against me. And so no wonder that I made it a necessary condition of my crossing the street.

The time had come when one might have supposed Cravath would have sorted out their problems with my case in some sensible way, but from what I had just heard from Mr. Sloan, it appeared that their posture had deteriorated into a number of haphazard positions and moves: no firm commitment to publish, no contract without a revoke, no date for starting or finishing the publishing procedure, no delivery date. Instead they would have Mr. Sloan "sell" me a new program in which I was to commit to six months, they month-to-month. This jabbing around had driven Mr. Sloan back on the fence and once again indefinitely extended the impasse.

# III

## Publication

## May 8, 1963–January 1964

Then, overnight, everything changed.

Barnum came to Eddie's office and announced that a "man from Detroit" had arrived and wanted to start the publishing process immediately. Eddie telephoned me: "They're so agreeable, it scares me."

In another day or so, Eddie and Barnum had resolved the stipulation problems that had long held them up. Mr. Sloan wrote to *Fortune,* saying it all as he closed his letter with: "I expect that such leave will be granted with the understanding that John afterward will return to *Fortune* without loss of his position." I delivered his letter to the publisher, Paine, and also my letter to the acting managing editor, Max Ways, requesting leave. Mr. Sloan asked Catharine to assemble an office staff to work on the closing. She reassembled several of her former stellar staff members, who years before had worked on the project. We brought onto our staff a high-performance copy editor, William Whipple, with whom I had worked on another book, *The Origins of Angling,* published by Doubleday in 1963 after heavy research but less tumult.

On Sunday, May 12, I wrote my lawyers telling them of the overnight change in General Motors' attitude toward the book. On Thursday afternoon, Friday, and Saturday, I had met with four General Motors staff executives and started to work on closing the gap on the book. The atmosphere was one of great cordiality, cooperation, candor, and speed of work. They came well prepared and under instructions from Donner to get it over with as fast as possible.

They had entirely withdrawn their revision of last fall, including the proposed changes to volume II, and made a relatively small number of points or requests, which they did not demand but urged on me, and then purely from the standpoint of technical legal problems.

In the first three sessions, we finished ten chapters of volume I with the exception of about eight "passes," problems that I wanted to reflect on before reaching a decision. Except for these "passes," I realized at the time that we could be through volume I by Monday night or Tuesday, and I would not have been surprised if we had completed both volumes within ten days.

They were agreeable to my bringing in a freelance copy editor from Doubleday to start work on what we had completed so that the manuscript could be ready for the printer when we were through. And unless we stumbled on the "passes," we would probably be ready to deliver the manuscript in June, or even, on the best estimation, late that month. This prospect was more of a surprise to me than it was to them. They were ready to start on page one and sail right through. They didn't want a new compact car chapter, and requested only that some supplementary material on the subject be added to the present text.

"The man from Detroit" was Daniel Boone (a descendant of the legendary pioneer), formerly their chief of litigation, on Al Powers's staff and currently close to Donner. He had retired, but had been brought back to function as special council for the case and to explain their legal problems to me. The Cravath attitude was wholly absent, which was puzzling.

Donner's orders for a quick resolution to the case had apparently reached Barnum, who I understood was preparing the Doubleday option contract to which I had objected. Cravath would still have to be watched for tricks in the contract, in light of the Time Inc. connection. I was concerned that their objective might be to strangle distribution of the book and subsidiary magazine rights (in 1959 they had rewritten the contract prepared by Matson in 1956, introducing weaknesses that I only now learned about).

I didn't know what Barnum was about to come up with, except that he wanted to spread the advance over five years and take the expected additional royalty over five years. He claimed that this was necessary for Sloan's tax purposes, but I wondered what he was really up to. I was willing to take the advance over five years, but I didn't want to decide on the rest until I had some idea of what to expect on additional royalty and subsidiary rights. This book could sell well or sell badly, depending on how it was handled given Doubleday's incentives rising from the contract and General Motors' attitude. Time Inc. had talked to me about coming back in with a series. I told them it should be published in *Life* as well as in *Fortune,* and that they should pay for publication in view of the fact that they had kept me at close to my 1954 salary. I told Paine that with two or three articles in *Fortune* alone, I would consider burial of the magazine rights.

We worked under a stipulation that once a book of which I approved was published, I would withdraw the suit. Mr. Sloan was to sign a binding contract by October 1. Donner had brought in Daniel Boone for the purposes of monitoring the process of publication and updating some factual data—such as a corrected chart of all GM car production since 1908.

Boone was a short man with a straight-up military bearing and a straightforward manner. The first thing he said to me when we first met, introduced by Bradley, I think, was to ask whether I would feel hostile toward him because of past hostilities surrounding the case. I said I recognized that as a lawyer he would represent his client, and that General Motors was known as a policy company; the policy that Boone brought was cooperation in publishing the book. If they, and he for them,

were prepared to cooperate in getting the book out without any
further delaying actions, I said I would not feel hostile toward
him. As it turned out, our relationship, while formal, was amiable and at times humorous. When he died not long after, his
wife wrote me that in his assignment to see the book through
he had had the best time of his life. Boone came each morning
from having stopped at Donner's office, sometimes with a message, as when Donner proposed changing the title of the book
from "The General Motors Story" to "My Years at General
Motors," a change I gladly accepted as more interesting, more
accurate, and less pretentious than our working title. Donner,
I imagined, was inspired by the perspective of "My Years,"
avoiding the appearance of leaving Donner, as current chief executive, only the administration of the principles of management that had been developed by Mr. Sloan; he had complained
of that impression of the book in a letter to Mr. Sloan in 1959.
I had occasionally wondered if that had had anything to do
with the suppression—lawyers finding a way to please the
C.E.O.—but I doubt it. Although our title had been only a
working title, Mr. Sloan, sensitive to seeming to be on an ego
trip, had no desire to change it. When I reported that to Boone,
he was so upset that, instead of waiting for another occasion
to discuss it, I went back into Mr. Sloan's office and said again
that it was a better title and that we had better accept it and
keep Moore out of it, or else. And he did.

Donner's two closest aides came to our office to provide factual information that I requested, but on our fourth day at
work, May 13, I learned that Donner and Bradley, in spite of
the assistance they had given us in the past and were giving us
now, preferred not to be listed among the many GM executives—living and dead—whose assistance Mr. Sloan and I

wanted to acknowledge. It was a list of credits like those rolled out at the end of present-day movies; it had indeed been a project of many hands, the last being my friend Walker Evans, who selected the photographs. The omission of Donner and Bradley didn't matter, but I asked Boone if their declining implied that GM was in some way going to bury the book. Boone said: "Absolutely not. We are over the divide. We are not going to litigate this book." I said, "Would you mind telling Cravath that? I think it would help with them." He responded, "I certainly will."

I asked him a hypothetical question: "If Mr. Sloan were to die before we published, and Tex Moore inherited control of the book and tried to stop its publication, what would you do about it?" He responded, "If he did that, don't worry, we'd sue him. I give you my word that you don't have to be concerned about that—it's not a risk." Since the March 20 meeting the real issue was whether GM accepted my proposition. Now, said Boone, speaking for Donner, they had.

Boone commented to me one day that General Motors would not have objected to the publication of the book had it been my book alone, but that as the book was being published by Mr. Sloan, an officer of General Motors, anything in the book could be put directly into evidence in a government suit against General Motors. Of course, if it had been my book alone, free of the parameters of Mr. Sloan's life and outlook, it would have been another book. Boone also said they had been unaware of the existence of the document, "Future Manufacturing Lines of The General Motors Corporation," with its Product Policy of 1921. This conversation was the closest I remember coming to the particulars behind the suppression, adding little but giving some support to my guess at the source of their anxieties. Boone never explained why he was called to take over from Cravath. This, together with Donner's takeover of the case with the sudden change of position, remained a puzzle.

I saw little of Cravath thereafter during the time of preparation and publishing, except on the magazine end where the great "white-shoe" law firm would reappear in the role of literary agent between Mr. Sloan and Time Inc., a change of hats that would not have been surprising had it been Moore's. The Cravath lawyers I knew on the other side of the case—Moore, Bromley, Barnum—seemed to like to present themselves as being in charge of things whether or not that was the way things were, their style being to dominate with modesty, to preside. This was truer of the senior pair. Barnum, who handled the day-to-day exchanges with Ennis in a lawyerly way, did a good job keeping things going without going anywhere, his apparent assignment. My impression of Cravath was of a polished *esprit de corps* that matched the esteem they were widely held in and were conscious of and which worked, within limits, until their operations got out of touch with elementary realities. Their persistent problem in my case, it seemed to me, was in the conflicts of interest between General Motors, Mr. Sloan, and Time Inc., following the lead of their senior partner and soon to be presiding partner, Maurice T. Moore, who was interested in Mr. Sloan's taxes but not in seeing the book published. In the last curious episode to come from this quarter, Mr. Moore did not appear on the stage, but he and Time Inc. were evidently out of touch, not realizing that General Motors and I had settled, and therefore still hostile to the book and its serialized publication in *Fortune*.

Barnum came in one day when we were working and went into Mr. Sloan's office. After a while he came out, stopped by and told me that Time Inc. would pay $15,000 for all serial rights, and was interested in two articles, possibly three in *Fortune*, but nothing in *Life* magazine. Barnum claimed that he had taken this up with Mr. Sloan, and that Mr. Sloan had agreed. When I asked how they had reached such an agreement, Barnum replied that he had put questions to Mr. Sloan and Mr. Sloan had given "affirmative" answers. That was pretty rank, and Barnum, who often spoke with candor while giving away nothing, said in answer to my question as to what this was all about: "Screw the writer, I guess."

Barnum's quip was true but not to the point. What was he doing here? Barnum had come to Mr. Sloan as an authorized agent representing whom? Time Inc.? Mr. Sloan? General Motors? One, two, or all? He had a pre-prepared deal with *Fortune* in hand, not for discussion but to be "affirmed" by Mr. Sloan. While the policy in this office was cooperation on the book, over at the Time and Life Building and downtown at Cravath, the policy evidently was noncooperation on the magazine series. They had sent Barnum here—he couldn't come on his own—to persuade, to order, or even to con Mr. Sloan into a deal that would cut back editorially and financially on the magazine series—in effect, taking full control of the serial rights to the book. They were not strong on selling the series, and so the series wouldn't sell the book. Something was wrong with this attitude. Time Inc.'s early enthusiasm for the series had not reawakened; on the contrary, they wanted to bury it discreetly. Did they not know the fight was over? Was it not? I would have to have another round with Time Inc. to break the Barnum-fronted deal. It took three steps, one with each of the principals in sequence: Mr. Sloan, Boone for General Motors, and Del Paine, publisher of *Fortune*.

Step one. I wrote my objections to the Barnum deal to Mr. Sloan in a memorandum dated May 31:

The trouble with Time Inc.'s proposal is that they want to buy all serial rights in perpetuity for a price far below a reasonable market price, or in any case without knowing the market price. Mr. Matson thinks the serial rights might be worth $50,000 or more. And besides, two articles in *Fortune* downgrades use of the book by *Fortune* from the four to six articles they formerly proposed to use. . . . I would almost rather withdraw the magazine rights from the market than to accept a downgraded proposal. The proposed Time Inc. arrangement spoils the magazine rights.

Mr. Sloan went home and telephoned me. He asked if I would come to his apartment. I found him extremely disturbed. He said he wanted to withdraw all magazine rights and not have any serial publication. No finessing of his responsibility. He would pay me for my share of the money loss. I said, "No, not yet. I work at *Fortune,* and I want it to be published there." I said I had an idea of what the trouble could be and asked him to wait until I had worked on it. He agreed to wait and see.

With that, the Barnum–Time Inc. deal with Mr. Sloan was dead, and so were the magazine rights if I could not come up with a better one. There was some obscurity about who was still around in this game, so—step two—I went to Daniel Boone and asked whether he had had anything to do with the matter, asking, in particular, whether General Motors had shown an interest in the magazine series. He said no, that General Motors was indifferent to it. He said, "Cravath represents General Motors only with regard to the stipulation. That has been settled." So Cravath had now made itself literary agent as well as lawyer for Time Inc. I then told Boone that I might be going to have a row with Cravath and Time Inc. and that whatever he heard about it and however it came out, he was not to worry, it would have nothing to do with us. Step three followed logically.

With General Motors out of the way, the thought I had about the magazine rights became quite simple. As a business proposition, the Cravath–Time Inc. proposal was too ridiculous to be strictly a business deal. It made no business sense to run down such a valuable property. It had to be something else that depressed the offer, and what else could it be but that Cravath and Time Inc. were living back in the Brownell era, in fear of General Motors and afraid that publishing Mr. Sloan was dangerous for Time Inc.? They were plugged into the Moore-Cravath connection to General Motors, unaware that it was no longer working. They were out of touch with reality, specifically the reality that while my lawsuit was still pending, everyone associated with the suppression, from Donner down, was determined to get it over with, by publication of the book. I went to see Del Paine and brought him up to date, explaining to him also that if *Fortune* did not improve its offer, Mr. Sloan would cancel the series.

In another overnight reversal *Fortune* then responded with a proposal for a five-part series (later six) for a total of $30,000, which was great editorially and tolerable financially. I advised Mr. Sloan to sign with *Fortune,* and he did.

Cravath's and Time Inc.'s joint blunder trying to ditch the Sloan magazine series throws a sidelight on the mystery of what had brought about General Motors' sudden change of position on the suit and the book. Demonstrably, from the moment the "man from Detroit" arrived, Cravath and Time Inc. were out of touch and soon out of date, as they were not participating in the settlement of the case.

With those institutions and their mastermind Moore set aside, and Mr. Sloan held on the fence, the cast of active players was reduced to three: Donner, Boone, and Bradley. Al Powers, though out of sight, was doubtless around for legal advice when called on, but Boone was carrying the ball for Donner. Donner, though formally the authority here, had never before been visibly active in the legal case, until near the end when he weighed in with the limit offer on my legal fees (which did not hold), and was personally unlikely to act alone in a matter concerning Mr. Sloan. That left Bradley, and there was as I saw it every reason for Bradley to be the one who took over and brought about the decision to publish the book in accordance with the proposal I had made. That Mr. Sloan back in January had proposed Bradley as his designated substitute on the case fitted this picture. However they got there, the way it ended was that Donner called in Boone as his special representative on the case and Boone, Bradley, and Donner and his aides became my only contacts as we moved toward publication.

Could it have been my proposal to eliminate the appendix, which contained several documents including the 1921 Product Policy, that caused GM's lawyers to agree to publication? The only other explanation that I could think of for General Motors' sudden change would be something external to my suit. For what it's worth, during the early 1960s General Motors reached its all-time peak and the Du Ponts cashed out their stock at the top of the market. More to the point could of course have been something to do with the Justice Department's antitrust investigation of General Motors, which was still ongoing and in its tenth year. On April 12, 1961, GM's Electro-Motive Division was indicted for monopoly in locomotives. Except for that case I can find no sign of antitrust action between the government and General Motors in the year 1963. During the time of their suppression of the Sloan book, Cravath defended General Motors against the antitrust actions—fending off and reducing the scope of subpoenas for documents, their legal defense based mainly on the Fourth Amendment forbidding unreasonable searches and seizures. But whatever happened there, that was outside the subject of the book.

We moved the manuscript rapidly through the publishing process in parallel activities in Mr. Sloan's office, at *Fortune,* and at Doubleday. Louis Banks, who would be *Fortune*'s next managing editor, skilfully extracted about 60,000 words out of the book's approximately 200,000 for the six-part series, which began in the September, 1963 issue. He used to say to me: "I would like to read 'My Years with Alfred P. Sloan.'"

*Fortune* commissioned Robert Weaver to produce a portrait of Mr. Sloan, who was the first person to appear on its cover. He sat for the portrait in a contemplative mood and when it came in, a nice painting, he complained to *Fortune:* "Why do you have to emphasize my disability?" He referred to the prominence of his hearing aid, which was clasped around his head. Weaver sympathized and painted it out. Doubleday asked Mr. Sloan for permission to use the portrait on the jacket of the book. When Mr. Sloan asked for this, Del Paine wrote him:

September 6, 1963
Dear Mr. Sloan:
*Fortune* is always happy to do you a favor. We will get in touch with Doubleday directly and inform them that they have our permission to use the portrait of you that appeared on the September cover.

Indeed, if you would like to have the original portrait, I would be honored to present it to you as a token of our long association in bringing "My Years with General Motors" to successful publication.

I trust you know that the first article in your series has already created extraordinary interest. For example, a friend of mine, William T. Young Jr., former president of Leo Burnett agency in Chicago, wrote me as follows:

"I have read almost everything about the great business personalities, from Robber Barons to the Fords, but never before has the reader had such a complete picture of what really goes on in a giant corporation. Mr. Sloan's modesty, too, is most appealing and strikes a new style in business reporting. He also gives due credit to Mr. Durant's contributions. This, to my mind, is long overdue. All in all the whole series should be great."

Needless to say, Mr. Sloan, *Fortune* is very proud to have these articles from a book which is destined to be regarded as one of the very few great histories of American enterprise.

Faithfully yours,
Ralph D. Paine Jr., Publisher
bcc:  Mr. Norton-Taylor
      Mr. Donovan
      Mr. McDonald

Happy to make the series its own publicly, *Fortune* put on a subscription promotion, which began:

FORTUNE, ALWAYS ALERT TO EDITORIAL ACCOMPLISH-
MENTS OF THE HIGH ORDER, BELIEVES THAT ITS READERS
WILL ATTACH THE GREATEST IMPORTANCE TO A NEW SE-
RIES OF ARTICLES WHICH WILL START IN THE SEPTEMBER
ISSUE, AND CONTINUE THROUGH JANUARY, 1964.
In these articles, unique in the literature of industrial management,
ALFRED P. SLOAN TELLS THE GENERAL MOTORS STORY to
be published next year as a book by Doubleday. . . .
WITH THIS ABSORBING DIVIDEND, YOUR *FORTUNE* SUB-
SCRIPTION WILL BE MORE VALUABLE THAN EVER.

In December of 1963, Doubleday had copies of the book in print and was shipping them to bookstores. General Motors paid my legal fees, and I ended my lawsuit. And so, in January, 1964, sixteen years after my first talk with Mr. Sloan, ten years after we started work on the book, five years after we completed it, and two years after I started suit against General Motors, the book, *My Years with General Motors* by Alfred P. Sloan, Jr., edited by John McDonald, with Catharine Stevens, was published. It was widely and favorably reviewed, was a best-seller on the *New York Times* list for about six months, was a strong seller in Japan, and was translated into seven other languages. Still in print as this is written, it remains a standard work on the automobile industry and corporate management.

About thirty-one years after the book's initial publication, on January 16, 1995, Bill Gates was quoted in *Fortune:*

I think Alfred Sloan's *My Years with General Motors* is probably the best book to read if you want to read only one book about business. The issues he dealt with in organizing and measuring, in keeping [other executives] happy, dealing with risk, understanding model years and the effect of used vehicles, and modeling his competition all in a very rational, positive way is inspiring.

When the book had appeared, Norton-Taylor approached me conspicuously at an office affair and thrust out his hand, saying: "Congratulations"—his public apology. Later at lunch he said, "You must feel triumphant." I replied that triumphant wasn't quite it, and to this day I wonder what it was.

# Epilogue

Lee Loevingel, assistant attorney general in charge of the U.S. Department of Justice's Antitrust Division in the 1960s, wrote to Dan Seligman in 1994 in response to his question concerning the upshot of the litigation against GM: "My best present recollection is that no case against GM charging monopoly in the automobile industry was ever filed."

# Index

Acheson law firm, 22, 76, 151

Adelman, Morris A., 13, 13n.1, 41

Advisory Committee, GM's, 1921 Product Policy of, 43, 46–49, 50. *See also* Product Policy of 1921

Agent, for *The General Motors Story,* 32. *See also* Matson, Arnold

Alexander, Henry C., completed draft reviewed by, 61

American Civil Liberties Union (ACLU), 78

Antitrust laws, 6, 7, 8, 50

AOL Time Warner, 4

Archive company, Du Pont as, 150

Auburn (automobile), 15

Automobile industry, ix, 148, 153, 154–155, 191

Automobile market, 7, 39, 43, 44, 45, 153, 163

Automobiles, 14, 15, 48. *See also specific models*

Barker, LeBaron R., Jr., 34

Barnum, John, 82, 105, 107, 109–110, 123, 124, 126, 129–130, 134, 138, 140, 141, 146–147, 157, 159–160, 165, 166, 168, 171, 177, 178, 182–183

"Big Three," 153

Black, Douglas, 53

Boone, Daniel, xi, 178, 179, 181, 184, 185–186

Bradley, Albert, 24, 43, 98, 106, 130–131, 180, 181, 185–186

Bradley's, Palm Beach, 27

Briscoe (automobile), 15

Bromley, Bruce ("Judge"), 4, 58–59, 75, 77, 81, 82, 86–87, 92, 98, 108, 109–110, 124, 148, 182

Bromley stipulation, 132

Brooks, George A., 83, 109–110, 156, 157, 164

Brown, Donaldson, 116

Brownell, Herbert, xi, 89, 89–90, 92, 93, 94, 95–96, 100–101, 105, 106, 108, 149

Budget, first book, 42. *See also*
    Contract; Gift; Royalties
Buick (automobile), 28, 50,
    153, 163

Cadillac (automobile), 28, 50,
    152, 153, 163
Cancellation, 37, 58–62
Carpenter, Walter, 24, 53, 61
Chalmers (automobile), 15
Chandler, Alfred D., 41, 43,
    118
Chevrolet, Louis, 29
Chevrolet (automobile), 28, 49,
    152, 153
Chevrolet Co., 29
Chief executives, risks taken
    by, 45. *See also* Executives,
    GM
Chrysler, Walter, xi, 5, 27, 28,
    30
Chrysler Corp., in oligopoly,
    153
Clayton Act, 50
Cohen, Elliot, 67
*Colliers,* 35
*Commentary,* 67
Contract, McDonald-Sloan, 16–
    19, 43, 44, 45, 107, 153,
    170. *See also* Settlement
Corporation, as economic insti-
    tution, 158
Cox, Ethylene, 75
Cox, Hugh, 22, 75–76, 79,
    151, 155
Cravath, Swaine, and Moore, x,
    4, 58, 75, 82, 97, 106, 125,
    133, 137, 139, 140, 148,
    164–165, 173, 178–179,
    182, 184, 185

Curtice, Harlow, 38, 51, 92
Custom-built cars, 48

Davis, Chester, xiii
Democratic Party, 26
Deposit of book, for later publi-
    cation, 120
Detroit, 14–15
Diesel locomotives, GM develop-
    ment of, 7
Disney, Walt, xiii
Dodge, Horace, 154
Dodge, John, 154
Dodges, the, 14
Donner, Frederic, 38, 52, 87,
    88, 91, 106, 109–110, 164,
    168, 169, 178, 180, 181,
    185–186
Donovan, Frank, 70–71, 76,
    77, 78, 79, 84, 90, 91, 92
Donovan, Hedley, 32, 33, 85,
    89, 93, 95
Dort (automobile), 15
Doubleday, 3, 33–34, 37, 38,
    53–57, 102, 111, 167–168,
    188
Doubleday/Currency, xiv
Dowd, Jack, 84, 85, 93
Drucker, Peter, xiv
Du Pont, Pierre, 22, 29, 30, 31,
    44, 53, 153
Du Pont Co., 9, 11–12, 18, 21,
    22, 24, 29, 37, 50, 51, 150
Du Pont trial, 50–51, 58, 60,
    75, 88
Durant, William C., 21, 28, 29,
    30, 44, 150, 163, 187

Economic crisis of 1919–1920,
    31

Edsel Fords, the, 14
*Education of Henry Adams,
The,* comparison with, 102
Eisenhower, Pres. Dwight D.,
27, 90
Eisner, Dorothy, 75
Electro-Motive Div., GM's, 186
Ennis, Edward J. ("Eddie"), xi,
75, 77, 78, 80, 81, 82, 87,
92, 94, 95, 101–105, 118,
119, 120, 121, 123, 124,
126–127, 129–130, 132,
134, 138, 140, 141, 168,
182
Epstein, Jason, 33
Essex (automobile), 15
Essex Coach (automobile), 49
Evans, Walker, xii, 181
Executives, GM, 61, 180–181
Exile, internal, 105

FBI, and Du Pont trial, 22, 51
"Federalist Papers, of American
Business, The," *The General
Motors Story* as, 115
Finance Committee, GM's, 30,
38
Financial policy, as foundation
of *General Motors Story,*
158–159
Fisher Body, 14
Fishers, the, 14
Fitelson, H. William (Bill), 77,
78, 94, 100–101, 118, 122,
139
Fitelson, Lasky, and Asian, 77–
78
Fitelson and Mayers, 71, 76,
77, 78, 121
Ford, Henry, 5, 154, 162n.3

Ford Motor Co., in oligopoly,
153
Fords, the, 14
Forster, Clifford, 77, 78, 80
Fortune 500, 6
*Fortune* magazine, xiv, 9–12,
15–16, 36, 56, 62–63, 80–
81, 81, 85, 87, 89, 105, 112,
113, 125–126, 132, 134,
179, 182, 185, 187, 188
*Fortune* staff, xii
Franchise dealers, 52
Furth, Bill, 81, 86, 90
"Future Manufacturing Lines of
the General Motors Corporation" (1921), 46, 181. *See
also* Product Policy of 1921

*Game of Business, The* (McDonald), xiii, 162n.3
Game theorists, 16
Game theory, xiii, 106–108,
162n.3
Garrison, John, 89, 90, 92, 94,
95, 101
Gates, Bill, ix–x, 189
General Motors Corp., x, 22–
23, 38, 39–40, 43, 79–80,
94, 97, 124–125, 184
antitrust investigation of, 90,
96, 186
basic car lines of, 49–50
chief objectives of, 47
concept of business of, 46–49
"copper-cooled" engine of, 43,
44, 45, 153
Du Pont investment in, 29–30,
150
early organization of, 22
executive committee of, 31

General Motors Corp (cont.)
    federal prosecutors and, 148
    Justice Dept. investigation of,
        37, 186
    leadership of, 158
    major policies of, 158
    objections to publication, 181
    in oligopoly, 153
    organization of, 51–52, 130
    in postwar automobile mar-
        ket, 7
    power hierarchy in, 52
    primary object of, 154
    proposals to, 123–124
    secretive nature of, 16
    Alfred Sloan's arrival at, 31
    Alfred Sloan threatened by,
        122
    stipulation of, 133–134
"General Motors Corporation/
    Organization Study," 21–22.
    *See also* "Organization
    Study"
General Motors legal team, 3, 4,
    82, 83, 105–106, 110–111,
    127–128, 141, 161–162,
    163, 165, 178–179, 182
*General Motors Story, The*
    (Sloan), 3, 13, 19, 23–24, 36,
    87, 98, 99, 135, 162, 160–
    161, 177. See also *My Years
    with General Motors*
    appendix to, 60
    cancellation of, 3, 4, 58–62
    Doubleday's characterization
        of, 102
    drafts of, xv, 28, 31–33, 52–
        54
    financial arrangements for,
        16–18

GM's fear of, 159–150
    introduction of, 36
    magazine rights to, 18–19
    Memorandum for Action with
        respect to, 110–111
    origins of, 12
    Product Policy chapter in, 152
    revised version of, 107
    two volumes planned for, 54–
        55
Getty, J. Paul, xiii
Gift, Alfred Sloan's (the trust),
    66–67, 84, 86, 88, 94, 103
Goldwater, Barry, 25
Graham, Billy, 26
Graham-Paige, 15

Harcourt Brace, response to first
    draft of, 33, 34
Hawkins, Norval A., 46
Haynes (automobile), 15
Hogan, Henry, 38, 50–51, 99,
    105, 148, 149, 150–151,
    155, 161
Hogan letter, 99, 102, 103
"Honorary Chairman," Alfred
    Sloan as, 24
"How to Get a Raise" (McDon-
    ald), 67
Hudson (automobile), 15
Hudson Motors, 49
Hughes, Howard, xiii
Humor, legal, 82
Hunt, Ormond E., 45–46
Hupmobile (automobile), 15
Hyatt Roller Bearings, 5, 30,
    31

Introduction, to *The General
    Motors Story*, 36

Jackson, Irene, 24
Jessup, Jack, 92
Justice Dept., Antitrust Div. of,
    4, 75

Kaysen, Carl, 13, 13n.1
Kettering, Charles, 4, 7, 29, 44–
    45, 46, 153
Klaxon horn, 31
Korean war, 9
Kucher, Miss., 27

La Rowe, Franklin, 109–110,
    111, 155, 156, 158
Legal expenses, McDonald's,
    167, 168–171, 186, 188
Legal teams. *See* General Mo-
    tors legal team; McDonald le-
    gal team; Time Inc. legal
    team
Leighton, George, 25
*Life* magazine, 35, 92, 179
Lincoln (automobile), 152
Linen, Jim, 89, 90, 91, 92
Locomobile (automobile), 15
Loevingel, Lee, 191
Lord, Day, and Lord, 89, 90–
    91, 92, 94, 97
Luce, Henry R. ("Harry"), x,
    32, 57–58, 85, 93, 101

Magazine rights, 87–88, 182–
    184, 185
Management, 1958 changes in
    GM, 51–52. *See also* Execu-
    tives
Market share, ceiling for, 7, 8
Market strategy, 45, 48, 152–
    153, 162n.3
Marmon (automobile), 15

Mason, Lowell B., 13n.1
Matson, Harold, 32, 33, 35, 36,
    54, 130, 184
Matson-Doubleday contract,
    167, 168, 170
Maxwell (automobile), 15
Mayers, Bertram (Bert), 77, 79,
    82, 94, 95, 97–99, 101, 109–
    110, 118, 121, 141, 144–
    147, 157
McCormick, Kenneth, 53, 57
McDonald, Christie, xiii
McDonald, Dorothy Eisner, xiii
McDonald, John, 19, 90, 91,
    94, 95, 96, 100, 101–102,
    104, 111, 112, 113, 114–
    116, 117–118, 123, 135–
    137, 136, 139, 167, 168, 172
  books produced by, xiii–xiv
  character of, xi
  Doubleday arrangements of,
    57
  as *Fortune* writer and editor,
    13, 15–16
  friends of, xii
  gambling of, xii–xiii
  as ghostwriter, ix
  legal fees of, 186, 188
  letter to Doubleday/Currency
    of, xvi
  politics of, xiii
  return to *Fortune,* 62
McDonald legal team
  agreements with GM team of,
    84, 86
  composition of, 77–78
  draft stipulation rejected by,
    140
  first meeting with GM's team,
    82

McDonald legal team (cont.)
July 14, 1962 correspondence
with, 97–101
meetings with Alfred Sloan,
109–110, 127–128
in negotiations, 121–122
objectives of, 79
and revision discussions, 117–
119, 120–121
in stipulations battle, 132,
138–139
and substitute author idea, 131
McDonald-Sloan correspon-
dence
Sept. 9, 1953, 11–12
July 29, 1956, 40
comments on proposed *Fortune* article, 10–11
January 23, 1960 letter, 65–66
March 5, 1962, 84
response to proposed revision,
114–116, 145
McDonald-Sloan meetings, 134
March 4, 1959, 3
December 14, 1962, 125
January 18, 1963, 134–137
March 12, 1963, 142–143
December 28, 1962, 127–128
McDonald suit, 92–93, 94, 106
and battle of stipulations, 127
beginnings of, 75
complaint sent, 81
early preparation for, 80
goal of, 79
grounds for, 86
nature of, 103
Alfred Sloan's reaction to, 108,
130
Meanings, deflected, of proposed revision, 116

Memorandum for Action, Sep-
tember 21, 1962, 110–111
Mendelsohns, the, 14
Miller, Joan McDonald, xiii
MIT
School of Industrial Manage-
ment, 8, 25
Alfred Sloan's graduation
from, 6, 30
Model T (automobile), 14, 15,
152, 154, 162n.3
Money concept, 154–155
Monopoly, 5, 76, 160, 161,
162, 191
Moore, Maurice T. ("Tex"), x–
xi, 4, 19, 37–38, 57, 59, 61,
62, 66, 67, 68, 69, 80, 84,
85, 86, 88, 91–93, 98, 108,
109–110, 117, 126, 128,
129, 130, 131, 132, 133,
137, 141, 160, 164, 181, 182
Morgan, J. P., 44
Morgan Bank, 30
Morgenstern, Oskar, xiii, 16
Motorcars, families and, 15. *See
also* Automobiles
Mott, Charles Stewart, 46
*My Years with General Motors*,
4. *See also The General Motors Story*
Drucker introduction for, xiv
jacket for, 187
main purpose of, xv
Product Policy of 1921 in, 49
Alfred Sloan's colleagues in,
xvi
strategies behind, x
success of, ix–x
title changed to, 180
working title for, 3

Nader, Ralph, 154
Nash, Charles W., 28
Nash (automobile), 15, 28
Nash Motor Co., 29
Negotiations, John McDonald's
 position on, 122. *See also*
 Stipulations, battle of
*New Yorker*, 16
*New York Intellectuals: The
 Rise and Decline of the Anti-
 Stalinist Left from the 1930s
 to the 1980s* (Wald), xiii
Nicholson, Harold, 93
Norton (publisher), 16
Norton-Taylor, Duncan, 62, 67,
 84–85, 88, 189

Oakland (automobile), 15, 28,
 49, 152
Olds, R. E., 15
Olds (automobile), 50, 152, 153
Oldsmobile (automobile), 15, 28
"Oligopoly," economic defini-
 tion of, 153, 153n.2
Operations committee, GM's, 30
Organization policy, as founda-
 tion of *General Motors Story*,
 158–159
"Organization Study" of 1919–
 1920 (Sloan), 21, 22, 31, 41
*Origins of Angling, The*
 (McDonald), 177
Overland (automobile), 15

Packard-Twin Six (automobile),
 15
Paige (automobile), 15
Paine, Ralph Delahaye, 67, 84,
 85–89, 95, 177, 179, 185,
 187, 188

*Paris Review*, 16
Parker, Sandy, 162
Pierce Arrow (automobile), 15
"Point Five," Raskob's, 50,
 150, 151
Poker, position play in, 106–
 107
Policy standards, GM's, 47
Pontiac (automobile), 28, 49,
 152, 153
Position play, in poker, 106–
 107
Postponement, 99, 100
Powers, Al, 105, 109–110, 140,
 142, 156, 164, 178, 185–186
Pratt, John, 116
"Price," GM's term, 49
Price classes, 152, 153
Price range, 48, 49
Price war, Chevrolet-Ford, 52
Product Policy document, as
 chapter 4, 162
Product Policy of 1921, 43, 46–
 49, 50, 76, 152, 154, 155,
 158–159, 161–162, 162n.3,
 163, 181
Progress reports, McDonald's,
 20, 23
Publication, 76, 77, 120, 165
Public interest, 79, 102, 103,
 121
Publishers, 32–34, 53. *See also*
 Doubleday
Publishing contract, in endgame
 meetings, 170. *See also* Con-
 tract
Publishing process, 177, 178,
 187
Publishing program, McDon-
 ald's, 171

Rainbow Room, 26
RAND Corp., 15
Raskob, John J., 26–27, 29, 30, 36, 50, 150, 151
REO (automobile), 15
Republican Party, 25
Research, GM's, 46
Research assistant, hiring of, 40–42. *See also* Chandler, Alfred D.
Revision, proposed, 110–111, 112, 113–116, 117–118, 119–120, 124, 135, 142, 147, 148, 157, 177
Roller bearing business, 5, 6, 30, 31
Royalties, 17–19, 149, 179
Rubin, Harriet, xvi

Salary, McDonald's *Fortune,* 67, 68
Sargent, John, 53, 57
*Saturday Evening Post,* 35
Saxon (automobile), 15
Schuster, Max, 35
Scripps-Booth (automobile), 15, 28, 49
Secretaries, Alfred Sloan's, 27, 138, 166
Seligman, Dan, 79, 105, 112, 191
"Senate Subcommittee on Concentration of Economic Power," 6
Settlement, 120–121, 155, 167, 168, 170, 185–186. *See also* Contract
Sheridan (automobile), 15, 28, 49
Sherman Antitrust Act, 7, 8

Simon and Schuster, response to first draft of, 33, 34, 35
Sloan, Alfred P., Jr., x, 131, 134, 156, 160
  agreement to publish of, 102–103
  ambivalence of, 18
  anecdotes, 26–27
  career of, 6
  education of, 6, 30
  elected GM president, 31
  endgame meetings with, 156–157, 164, 166, 167
  *Fortune* article planned by, 10
  GM's threat to, 122
  and John McDonald's compromise
  loyalties of, 27
  market strategy of, 162n.3
  meetings about meeting with
  memoirs of, ix
  at October 1962 meeting, 109–110
  offices of, 6, 8
  personality of, 3, 18, 26
  politics of, 25
  pressure on Cravath by, 165
  problems with deafness, 113, 125, 127–128, 134
  proposed revision and, 113
  reaction to John McDonald's compromise, 161
  resignation of, 24
  secretaries of, 27, 138, 166
  in stipulations battle, 133
  successor to authorship of, 129–130, 181
Sloan, Raymond, xv, 24–25, 130

Sloan Foundation, 8, 25, 59, 108
Sloan-Kettering Medical Center, 4, 8, 25
Sloan-McDonald correspondence, 11, 63–64, 83
Solow, Herbert, 87
Sources, checking, 39
Spellman, Cardinal, 26
Stevens, Catharine, 3, 23, 24, 26, 28, 39, 41, 53, 60, 142, 146, 159
background of, 20
closing staff assembled by, 177
Doubleday arrangements of, 57
expanding role of, 42
at March 20, 1963 meeting, 157
Matson's auction and, 34
Moore's opposition to, 145
at project beginning, 19–20
proposed revision and, 108, 112–113, 118, 135, 156
as Sloan's general assistant, 61–62
and stipulations battle, 127, 143
Stevens, Roger, xii
Stipulations, battle of, 121, 140, 144. *See also* Revision, proposed
absence of particulars in, 147
arranging meetings during, 143–144, 145, 146
Cravath, Swaine, and Moore in, 125, 133, 137, 140, 164–165
first proposal to GM in, 123–124

GM's position in, 124–125, 133–134
John McDonald's summation of, 134–137
Moore's proposal in, 132
resolution of, 177
Alfred Sloan's reaction to, 126
strategy in, 139
substitute for Sloan designated, 129
Storch, Miss, 138, 166
*Strategy in Poker, Business, and War* (McDonald), xiii–xiv, 16
Studebaker (automobile), 15
Stutz Bearcat (automobile), 15
Subsidiary rights, 179. *See also* Magazine rights
"Summit" meetings, 109, 142–143
Summons, served on GM, 83, 86, 105
Suppression effort, GM's, ix, xi, xiv, 5, 76, 79, 81–82, 86, 95–96, 97, 98, 99, 100–101, 102, 103, 104–105, 108, 114–116, 149–150, 157–158, 181
Supreme Court, N.Y., McDonald suit in, 123–124, 133–134
Supreme Court, U.S., 37
adverse ruling of, 58
Du Pont case in, 50, 98

Tape recorder, Sloan's use of, 20
Texaco-Pennzoil-Getty litigation, 79

*Theory of Games and Economic Behavior* (von Neumann and Morgenstern), xiii
Time Inc., x, 4, 172
  advertising interests of, 85, 86–87, 91, 94
  and final settlement, 185
  magazine rights of, 19
  McDonald suit and, 80, 81
  neutrality of, 85, 87, 112
  outside counsel for, 88
  public relations interest of, 87–88
  and serialization rights, 183
  suit delayed by, 83, 84
Time Inc. legal team, 84–85, 89, 94, 95
Title, 3, 113, 180
Trigger theory, 150–151, 155, 161
Trotsky, Leon, xii
Trust fund, Sloan's proposed gift of, 59, 66, 69. *See also* Gift

United Automobile Workers, 14
United Motors, 30, 31

Volume I, 54–55, 158, 159
Volume II
  planning for, 54–55, 158
  revised, 171
von Neumann, John, xii, xiii, 16

Wald, Alan M., xiii
*Wall Street Journal,* 92
Warren, Eleanor Clark, 75
Warren, Robert Penn, xii, 75
Water-cooled engine, 45, 154

Ways, Max, 112, 177
Weaver, Robert, 187
Whipple, William, 177
Wills, C. Harold, 15
Wills Saint Claire (automobile), 15
World War II, 7, 25

Young, William T., Jr., 187

Zeckendorf, William, xii